What Will They Think of Next . . .?

What Will They Think of Next . . .?

Unpublished Letters to
The Daily Telegraph

EDITED BY
IAIN HOLLINGSHEAD

Aurum
Press

First published 2014 by
Aurum Press Limited
74-77 White Lion Street
London N1 9PF
www.aurumpress.co.uk

A catalogue record for this book is available from the British Library.

ISBN 978 1 78131 291 9

10 9 8 7 6 5 4 3 2 1
2018 2017 2016 2015 2014

Typeset in by SX Composing DTP, Rayleigh, Essex

Printed and bound in Great Britain by CPI Group (UK) Ltd,
Croydon, CR0 4YY

SIR — Forget the front page and all the pages in between, I always turn straight to the letters, where I know I will find enlightenment, amusement and teeth-grinding irritation.

Pity it is so short.

John Pearson
Hove, East Sussex

SIR — Yesterday my hernia was repaired painlessly under general anaesthetic. This morning I started on your publication *Imagine My Surprise . . .* I read just seven letters before the scintillating wit caused me to laugh so hard I imagined my stitches might burst. There was no alternative but to put down your hilarious compendium.

Now much looking forward, when stronger, to this and the other publications.

Crombie Glennie
Hawksworth, Nottinghamshire

SIR – The letters books are a great source of amusement, but I had to remove them from my downstairs loo as guests were of the same opinion. I wondered why they remained in situ for so long, and I have now had to banish the books to the upstairs loo.

Margaret Wilson
Hungerford, Berkshire

SIR – Ukraine is in turmoil, a plane inexplicably vanishes, many farms remain flooded, an asteroid comes close to earth, and you publish a letter about spilling grains from a sugar packet. Get a grip!

Barry McCartney
Sudbury, Suffolk

CONTENTS

INTRODUCTION

Is there a conspiracy on Fleet Street to keep women off the Letters pages? I'm writing this just after discussing the topic on the *Today* programme with the charming John Humphrys (you might notice the lack of rude letters about him this year). It transpired that someone with far too much time on their hands had counted all the letters to the *Financial Times* over a three-week period and just three were written by women. Frankly, the more surprising revelation for me was that the pink paper had a Letters page. After all, where's the fun in debating the FTSE compared to swapping tips on how best to swing bowl an unwanted snail round a tree and into a neighbour's garden?

There is, of course, no conspiracy. The letters editors at *The Daily Telegraph* are gender blind, colour blind and even county blind, despite occasional accusations that we only print letters from Dorset. One of my favourite ever letters could only have been written by a woman: 'Fifty shades of grey . . . succinctly describes my lingerie collection.' It is true that men write some 75 per cent of our letters, a handful of them writing two or three times a day. Men are, perhaps, more prone to being gloriously and eccentrically alone in thinking the way they do.

And they tend to write the more outlandish missives, such as the retired lieutenant colonel in these pages who likes to go naked, save for his regimental tie, or the chap who declined sexual favours from his wife so that he could win at Scrabble — and then sat down to write a letter to a newspaper to tell everyone about it.

However, the criteria for publication are the same whether you're Lieutenant Commander Joe Bloggs (retd) from Blandford Forum, Dorset or Josephine Bloggs from Dobcross, West Yorkshire. Men appear to enjoy writing about the dishwasher just as much as women enjoy writing about the World Cup. And thankfully for the rest of us, both sexes seem equally prepared to share their spouses' failings with the world at large. Have there ever been better glimpses into a marriage than the letters here which start: 'I often chastise my wife for mistakenly using the word *bought* instead of *brought*...'; or 'I simply do not understand why my husband was not chosen for one of the teams competing in the World Cup...'?

In the early hours of the morning I sometimes worry whether the paper's wonderful legion of loyal letter writers, whether male, female or of indeterminate initialled gender, will be able to keep it up year after year. I am always put to shame. This year, the sixth in a row, is, I believe, a particularly bumper crop. There is no subject too weighty not to be punctured with their ready wit, no topic too trivial not to be treated with the ironic seriousness it deserves. How can we halt Russian aggression in Ukraine? Frustrate the President with a subscription to TalkTalk. How can François Hollande preserve his anonymity during his romantic trips around Paris? Borrow a Boris bike from the London Mayor. Where do all the beautiful women go when the sunshine vanishes? No one seems to know. This was the year of Putin and Paxman, Sharon and Suarez, Harris and Hollande and, thankfully, for the first time since these books began, not a single letter about Gordon Brown.

I am grateful, as ever, to Christopher Howse, the Letters Editor, for his unfailing support; Matt Pritchett, for another wonderful cover cartoon; Cerys Hughes, publishing manager at the *Telegraph*; and everyone at Aurum. I must make special mention of Sally Peck on the letters desk who has again taken on the enormous task of sifting through tens of thousands of offerings. The book would not have been possible without her expert eye.

My largest debt of gratitude is, of course, to all the letter writers for their wonderful company – with perhaps a special mention for M, the correspondent who believes himself in charge of MI6, but actually writes from an internet cafe in Bristol. After a break from duty last year, he returns to form to share his thoughts on the Syrian crisis.

This year finds his competition on similarly fine form. Whether explaining UKIP's rise through the horrors of Eurovision, wondering how to insure the Lamborghini on which they might blow their pension pot or sharing their naughty mnemonics to remember the cranial nerves of a dogfish, one thing is certain: no one has any idea what they will think of next.

I can't wait to find out.

Iain Hollingshead
London SW11
August 2014

FAMILY LIFE AND TRIBULATIONS

A COLD FRONT

SIR – For days now you have forecast dark clouds and lightning over Gloucestershire while the weather has been generally sunny and warm. Are you actually forecasting an unplanned visit by my mother-in-law? Please clarify.

Martyn Dymott
Gloucester

(NOT SO) MANY YEARS FROM NOW

SIR – When I switch on my hearing aids they play the first four notes of the Beatles song 'When I'm 64'. I really do not need a daily reminder.

D.A. Cameron
Othery, Somerset

SIR – You report that any alcohol consumption increases the risk of dementia. What if I forget not to have a drink?

Brian Farmer
Chelmsford, Essex

SIR – You report that scientists have found that sex can be as beneficial as playing sport, going for a strenuous walk or jogging. Was I alone in hiding the newspaper from my husband today?

Kirsty Blunt
Sedgeford, Norfolk

SIR – I recently celebrated my 60th birthday. My dear wife's present to me was a new 'health band'. Its principal function appears to be to send an alert to my wife's iPad whenever I sit still for longer than 12 minutes.

She assures me this guarantees I will live to a ripe old age. Isn't progress wonderful?

J.C.
London SW6

SIR – In a supermarket queue I was asked how old my accompanying grandchildren were – an endearing question, had they not been my children.

Piers Casimir-Mrowczynski
Gustard Wood, Hertfordshire

SIR – During a casual chat with my GP in a recent routine check-up, he informed me that statistically the most dangerous time for a human is the first four months of life. I put it to him that the figures for the last four months aren't terribly encouraging either.

Martin Henry
Good Easter, Essex

SIR – Walking in a Brighton street I was surprised when an elderly lady going in the opposite direction muttered, 'You sexy beast.' I am 81. It made my day.

Richard Pitcairn-Knowles
Otford, Kent

HOW TO BE A MAN

SIR – Last Saturday I attended the much talked about 'Being a Man' Festival, where I discovered to my horror that most of the conversation presupposed that 90 per cent of males spend 90 per cent of their time viewing hardcore porn. Manliness as a topic was shunted aside in favour of a feminist agenda that made room only for partisan grievances against the Great White Male.

The final session of the day focused on Ordinary Blokes – like plumbers. Each of the three self-avowed non-blokey panellists struggled hard to describe a way he had experienced the blokiness that is so typical of the plumbers unrepresented on the panel.

Fortunately, this was soon submerged by Billy Bragg's diatribe promoting his favourite causes. In this regard the entertainer showed himself to be an outstanding man, for what real man is not intoxicated by the sound of his own voice?

The day descended into farce when a woman who had been hanging around all day mounted the stage to screech about the evils of white male dominance. She finished her rant by reading a 'Man's Bill of Rights', which was so neurotic it could only have been written by a girl. I was wrong. It had been penned by Grayson Perry.

This show was intellectually vapid, culturally revisionist, politically cloistered and a waste of twelve quid. I blame Jon Snow. I only went because he did.

Next year I'll go to the pub and watch the game with the plumbers.

A.D.
Hastings, East Sussex

SIR — I read with interest your report that the R&A Golf Club is expected to admit women members. How about some equality for men? The Women's Institute, YWCA, Girl Guides, maternity leave, Mums and Tots Clubs — none are for men.

I don't expect you to print this letter because we are not pink and lovely like mothers.

Richard Tovey
London SE18

SIR – On July 10, 1983 I was captaining my cricket team in a match just outside Newbury while my wife was in the second day of labour with our daughter Alice in the Princess Margaret Hospital, Swindon.

This splendid child delayed her arrival long enough for me to finish the game, have some necessary post-match beers, and still arrive in time to support my wife at the birth.

Women will have babies quite successfully whether the father is present or not.

Roy Bailey
Great Shefford, Berkshire

SIR – I read that psychologists have concluded that there is little difference between the sexes, and that men and women think in virtually the same way. I can only assume that the researchers involved are unmarried.

P.G.
Poole, Dorset

SIR – When I married, 48 years ago, my bride and I, as naturists, were clothed as were Adam and Eve. The priest, a fellow naturist, was similarly naked. Give or take the odd wrinkle, our wedding attire has been in daily use as foundation garments, topped invariably, in my case, by a regimental tie.

Lt Col A. St John-Grahame (retd)
Whitstable, Devon

SIR – A gentleman without a tie is neither properly dressed, nor is he a gentleman.

Arthur W.J.G. Ord-Hume
Guildford, Surrey

SIR – Many years ago I was in a hospitality marquee at an air display at RAF Fairford. With a glass in one hand and a plate of food in the other, I was still wearing my Panama hat when a man in front of me turned and, looking at the dark blue and red ribbon, asked: 'Brigade of Guards?'

Without thinking, I replied, 'No, Marks and Spencer.' The poor chap was overcome with embarrassment, and so was I.

David Carrick
Petersfield, Hampshire

SIR – Never mind ties, when are men going to start wearing tights again? That's what I want to know.

Hugh Bebb
Sunbury on Thames, Middlesex

SILKY SEXUAL CONCERNS

SIR – Whenever I see the word *denier*, I think of ladies' silk stockings. I am well into my eighth decade. Should I be concerned?

John Gibson
Standlake, Oxfordshire

SIR – On Saturday you quoted Nigella Lawson saying that she enjoyed hosting dinner parties where there would be 'nobody coming that I would be uncomfortable in front of just wearing socks and leggings and no make-up'.

If she was to host a party dressed like that I do not think many of the male guests would notice the lack of make-up.

John Currie
Lanark, Lanarkshire

SIR — As I view the numerous beautiful women walking about in the sunshine I have to ask, where do they all go in the winter?

P.W. Tibbs
King's Lynn, Norfolk

SIR — A rather attractive lady walked into our golf club lounge the other day wearing a shirt with Ping embroidered on it. I was about to suggest that wearing such a word over her bra strap was asking for trouble but then thought better of it.

J.P.
Suckley, Worcestershire

SIR — You report that 'four in ten 16-year-old girls never undertake any vigorous physical activity'. I have a suspicion that they do.

A.C.
Bridport, Dorset

SIR — The best contraceptive is an aspirin, held between the knees.

Diana Hogge
Clyst St George, Devon

SIR — More moons ago than I care to remember, a Valentine's card arrived containing a small package. On the card was written: 'Roses are red, Violets are blue, Mine's Pink, with love to Huw.'

I unwrapped the package: it was a small leather case marked, 'Working Man's Brief Case'. Inside were three coloured condoms. It was from a particularly witty girlfriend.

These days, with my condom days no longer even in my rear-view mirror, I use it as a holder for my visiting card. When I whip it out to present someone, folk always notice the case and the tale is told.

Huw Beynon
Llandeilo, Carmarthenshire

PS Size really matters: I attach a photo of said brief case — a 50 pence coin offers up a sense of proportion (mind you, I'm not sure the Queen is amused at being used as a reference point).

SIR — Sex after 50, asks your report? I should say so! My partner and I are in our late seventies and still enjoy a stimulating and fulfilling sex life. Long may it continue!

PLEASE DO NOT PRINT MY NAME
Ilfracombe, Devon

SIR — When Susannah Reid talks about 'great chemistry' I take it she means the kind that fizzes vigorously and then explodes, leaving behind a nasty smell and lots of mess.

Felicity Thomson
Symington, Ayrshire

SIR — The proposed Islamic ban on sex education in schools is all for the good. One of the reasons I left teaching was weariness over constantly having to blow up condoms and poke them round the room, instead of teaching the three Rs.

W.S.
London N17

SIR — The man charged with having sex in the charity shop had obviously 'shopped around' and found it to be cheaper than the brothel next door.

Joanne Lawson-Chilcott
Portbury, Somerset

MILK, NO SOUL

SIR – On entering a cafe in Glasgow a few years ago, I was asked, 'What can I get you, sonny?' by a chirpy young woman who was at least 30 years younger than me.

'Can I please have a sausage and egg sandwich and do you have any Earl Grey?' I asked.

She popped away for a minute or so. On her return she said: 'Son, you can have a sausage and egg sandwich, but we don't play soul music in here.'

Fergus Anderson
London SW6

SIR – I bought two pots of home-made jam at a local market recently, the jars both marked at £1.50. The charming young lady in charge didn't have a calculator, so I waited patiently while she called a friend on her mobile phone to check the total purchase price.

Sandra Hawke
Andover, Hampshire

SIR – I have urged the captains of two major food retailers to try to open any of their shrink-wrapped fish and meat products without damaging the merchandise inside or cutting their fingers using the sharp implements required: knife, scissors, screwdriver, bradawl, chisel or knitting needle.

None have replied.

Terry Burke
Canterbury

SIR – Would the person whose idea it was to put thin condoms on fat cucumbers please stand up?

Philomena Smart
Ewell, Surrey

SIR – Am I alone in mourning the demise of the age of innocence? Recent visits to sugar confectionery shops in popular seaside resorts have failed to locate a single rock kipper. There was no shortage of seaside rock moulded into more explicit shapes, which I will leave to readers' imagination.

George Plume
Ipswich, Suffolk

SIR – Since the Toys 'R' Us outlet at the new retail park in Sydenham in South London sells toys, should I alert the authorities that the adjacent store is called Babies 'R' Us?

Michael Stanford
London SE23

CINDERELLA'S SLIPPER REVENGE

SIR – This new Cinderella Law is very interesting. I wonder if it has any retroactive provisions. My mum hit me when I was seven years old and I have been waiting many years to get back at her.

C.L.
Tullibody, Clackmannanshire

SIR – Under the Cinderella Law parents who starve their children of affection would be prosecuted. But how to define emotional cruelty?

I once said to my young son: 'I only hope that when you grow up you will have children just like you.'

He burst into tears and cried, 'Oh, you are a cruel mummy.'

Beatrice Baxter
Ilford, Essex

SIR – If children will be able to sue their parents when dissatisfied with their upbringing, will parents have equal rights to sue offspring who have not lived up to their expectations?

Dennis Peirson
Ventnor, Isle of Wight

SIR – I thought we already had a Cinderella Law, recently enacted to permit the Ugly Sisters to 'marry' each other.

Michael Cleary
Bulmer, North Yorkshire

SPARE THE ROD, SPARE THE MOTHER

SIR – Returning home after school, my generation did not shout, 'I shagged your mum' out of train windows. It's not because we were truthful or weren't horrible; it's because some nearby adult would have given us a good clout over the lug, fully supported by our hotly embarrassed parents and disgusted head teachers.

Michael Rolfe
Cape Town, South Africa

SIR — If parents welcome the demise of the name tape, teachers may not. Being caught in the act by an unfamiliar teacher, it was a popular wheeze to give a false name, preferably of an unsuspecting classmate. A suspicious teacher could execute a quick, rather robust, manoeuvre to reveal the name tape on the back of the culprit's collar, and therefore their true identity.

Dominic Weston Smith
Fernham, Oxfordshire

SIR — At my prep school in the Home Counties in the early 1960s, corporal punishment was administered with a garden cane on bare bottoms by the headmaster.

Following punishment, the school doctor would be summoned to extract bamboo splinters from the victim.

Andrew H.N. Gray
Edinburgh

THE GREATER ESCAPE

SIR — One naturally hopes that the teenage runaway Stonyhurst sweethearts are safe and well.

Their plight on a beach in the Dominican Republic is a far cry from similar escapades during my 10-year spell (1972-82) at the College.

We too had occasional breakouts during the miserable and bleak winters. These involved eschewing all forms of motorised transport, trekking for miles across farmland and fell to Clitheroe or Preston, posing as chimney sweeps and actuaries to evade sharp-eyed, dog-collared Jesuits as they scoured the railway platforms, and desperately searching for a locomotive to the sanctuary of choice for escapees: Blackpool.

A baseball glove and solitary awaited your inevitable return.

Now it is a pre-booked taxi and cheap flights to the Caribbean. Perhaps we are witnessing another unintended consequence of quantitative easing and the low interest rate environment.

Jonathan Kelly
London SW12

SIR – Stonyhurst College is not all doom and gloom. A former headmaster once told how a prospective parent was being shown the corridor on which the 11-year-old boys did their prep. Every study space was plastered with posters of Page Three girls, except for one, which had pictures of expensive cars.

'Why have you got pictures of cars?' he asked the occupant.

'Well, Sir, my father sells cars,' came the reply. 'And you might very well wonder what the other boys' fathers sell.'

Kevin Heneghan
St Helens, Lancashire

FREE AT THE POINT OF OBESITY

SIR – After 50 years of smoking, I have finally kicked the habit, thanks to e-cigarettes. I am now obese. Can I expect the NHS to fund my membership of Weight Watchers?

Diana Whiteside
Berkhamsted, Hertfordshire

SIR — There are many countries with starving people. Let us export the porkies for them to eat — a win-win situation, with no drain on the NHS, a small charge for airfares and a reduction in foreign aid.

Alan Kibblewhite
Blandford Forum, Dorset

SIR — Critics have been brutal about the size of the Irish opera singer Tara Erraught. My favourite story is of an amateur production of *Rigoletto*, in which Rigoletto's daughter Gilda was played by a lady of alarming proportions. In the last heart-rending scene, where a sack containing Gilda's corpse must be dragged offstage by her father, a voice from the back row was heard to say, 'I think you may have to make two trips.'

Jane Cullinan
Padstow, Cornwall

SIR — The fattest man in England in the second half of the eighteenth century was reputedly Dr Phillip Hayes, known appropriately as 'Fill Chaise'. He was Professor of Music at Oxford University.

The diarist John Marsh recounts a visit to Canterbury Cathedral in 1784: 'We all went to the evening service when Dr Hayes again played the organ, who being (as is well known) a very large man, it was doubted by many whether he would after all be able to get up the narrow winding staircase to the new organ loft without sticking by the way, to ascertain which it was actually measured when it appeared that there would be full room for his carcass and that it would be unnecessary to hoist him up in a chair withoutside by a crane.'

Ian Graham-Jones
Emsworth, Hampshire

SIR – A casual glance at the percentage of people who are overweight shows that it increases as we get older. To put it another way, the percentage of people who are not overweight decreases, suggesting that it is they who are dying early.

Les Sharp
Hersham, Surrey

SIR – One frequently reads in your pages that the NHS faces problems caused by an 'ageing population'. Show me one that isn't, and I'll gladly join it.

Michael Hayes
Wetheral, Cumbria

SIR – I read that the pollution on Wednesday was as bad as it gets. Are you all dead?

Dave James
Tavistock, Devon

SIR – Given the ease with which the maximum of 10 on the air pollution scale was reached we need a new measure. Footballers would appreciate 110 per cent, guitarists would enjoy 11 and teachers an A*.

Michael Powell
Tealby, Lincolnshire

POOH CORNER

SIR – Having been invited by the NHS to participate in their 'bowel cancer screening test', I can imagine that many people are put off by the name, as well as by the procedure itself.

Considering the age-group in question, many of us are familiar with the wonderful books of A. A. Milne concerning a certain bear and his friends, and in particular a game they played on the bridge over the stream. So perhaps naming the bowel test 'Pooh sticks' would make it less intimidating and ensure a better uptake.

John F. Roberts
Amersham, Buckinghamshire

SIR – Many hospitals provide newspapers in waiting rooms. This compassionate gesture is welcomed by those who – as was the case for me today – occasionally forget to bring their own *Daily Telegraph*.

Imagine my alarm this morning, then, at finding that the only newspaper available in a busy waiting room – and this is very difficult to relate – was an unopened copy of the *Guardian*.

I can recall times when, on reading this newspaper, I have found myself losing the will to live.

> S.L.G.
> Wirral

SIR – I congratulate anyone who can get a doctor appointment quickly. Our surgery operates a triage system: if you are nearly dead, you can usually be seen the day you 'phone, as long as that is before 9 a.m., you can get through, and you can get to the surgery to be seen.

> P.F.
> Halesworth, Suffolk

SIR – The Health Police want us to upgrade from five portions of fruit and vegetables a day to seven or even ten. Given the inevitable effect of a high-fibre diet on the bowels, that means at least three visits to the lavatory per day. Yet our culture is unfriendly to frequent toileting. That leads many actively to avoid high-fibre meals for fear of having to go in the middle of a meeting or theatrical performance.

If we are to become full-time frugivores, we need to become less hostile to number twos. To need a poo outside the home should not be a source of shame or embarrassment; it could be saving our lives.

Anthony Rodriguez MA BSc Health Sciences (Hons, First class)
Staines Upon Thames, Middlesex

LOOS WITH A VIEW

SIR – I found a 'stereo', double-seat lavatory here in darkest France, lurking in a pigeon tower. Having discovered this peculiar arrangement I got to thinking about who could possibly qualify to share such a personal moment. I failed.

Vincent Hearne
Nabinaud, Poitou-Charentes, France

SIR – While reluctant to be considered an expert on the subject of latrines, as we called them in the RAF during the war, it should be noted that a double-seat closet is hardly exceptional to an ageing veteran. On arrival in Egypt one was confronted by a building which housed at least a dozen units in a large circle, separated by about a metre, outside of which I would wait, sometimes for long periods in great discomfort, until there was a vacancy at an acceptable distance from other occupiers.

Bert Gladwin
Nash, Buckinghamshire

SIR – The view from the loo at the Shard restaurant, on the 32nd floor, is unsurpassed; my friend calls it 'le piss de resistance'.

H.N.
Tonbridge, Kent

SIR – The correspondence regarding loo rolls reminds me of an age when such luxuries were not universal.

Years ago I was appointed manager of a farm buildings company in the heart of rural England and one of my duties was the management of the advertising budget.

One day the representative of a local weekly paper called on me. Present at this meeting was our sales manager, a lugubrious, pipe-smoking man who lived nearby in a small cottage with minimal facilities.

The representative turned to him and said: 'You take *The Advertiser*, don't you?'

His reply has stayed with me ever since: 'Not any more – we have a water closet now.'

Sid Davies
Bramhall, Cheshire

SIR – When I started work at The National Trust's Regional Office at Lanhydrock in Cornwall in 1980, I found that the legendary regional director insisted on having two types of toilet roll: soft, labelled boy's, and hard, labelled men.

Phillip Hunt
Saltash, Cornwall

THE GREAT UNWASHED

SIR – When large passenger ships were 'liners' not 'cruise ships', the cabin stewards were British menservants who gave impeccable service. A former first class cabin steward told me of an elderly gentleman travelling to Australia in an Orient Liner who had booked the sole use of a large suite with a private bathroom.

On embarkation the steward asked the passenger: 'At what time would you like your bath, sir?'

The old man replied: 'Friday, please.'

Nelson French
Fordingbridge, Hampshire

SIR – As a former Scout leader of many years, I was taught the importance of a soap inspection before the return home: all bars were to be removed from their wrapping and suitably distressed in order to simulate a week's washing.

It is well known that while you can lead a Scout to water, you cannot make him wash.

A.C.
Willingham, Cambridgeshire

SIR – Your correspondent's complaint about the cleanliness of beards led me to investigate my own. She has a point; it contained a pheasant and two woodcock which had chosen to hide there during a nearby shoot last month. They had survived on odd bits of dribbled food, presumably. I released them to the wild.

Peter McKenzie
Morpeth, Northumberland

SIR — My wife says that the reason I have a beard is to let people know where my head stops and my neck begins.

Simon Pike
Hoarwithy, Herefordshire

OVERCHARGED

SIR — My wife and I have been preparing to spend a week in a small cottage on the North Yorkshire coast. I have packed nine chargers for items of essential electrical equipment, ranging from a smart phone through to a toothbrush. I also have a 10th charger but have no idea what it charges so that will be coming with us, just in case.

Is this normal?

Jeff Jaycock
Harrogate, North Yorkshire

SINISTER TOOTHPASTE

SIR — When I was a lad, the only reading material I was allowed at the breakfast table was the cornflake packet.

In later years I came to realise that the only readily available reading material while I was brushing my teeth was the toothpaste tube. Alas, as a right-handed person, when I have put the tube, which I have in my left hand, onto the shelf, the printing on it is upside down.

Will toothpaste makers please produce tubes for right-handed people?

Bruce Chanter
Potters Bar, Hertfordshire

SIR – As a left-handed writer, the advent of the ballpoint pen couldn't come quickly enough. However, waiting for the ink to dry gave me plenty of time to think.

Tony Baker
Edinburgh

SIR – It appears that all Y-Front underpants are right-handed.

Tony Eaton
Northallerton, North Yorkshire

KITCHEN HOOLIGANS

SIR – The delight at the installation of a new kitchen wears very thin. Guests invited to the opening supper, where I endeavoured to show my culinary skills, were assaulted with microwave beeps, oven pings, moans from a kettle with five different coffee temperatures, a series of five sets of three rings from a dishwasher, beeps from an induction hob that insists no object covers its controls, and a whistle from my husband's hearing aid, which got totally confused listening to all the other sounds.

I hadn't learned to silence all these kitchen hooligans.

Celia Timmington
Southport, Merseyside

SIR – My dishwasher neither beeps nor pings when he has finished the washing-up.

Clare Byam-Cook
London SW15

MANNERS MAKETH OFFICER

SIR – I read with interest and sympathy the comments of Major General James Cowan regarding manners in the Officers' Mess. They reminded me of the senior living-in member of our Mess in Catterick who, in 1967, banned baked beans because they were 'not an officer's vegetable'.

It is only in recent years that my digestive system has told me why he considered them so unsuitable.

R.S. Hoe
Pockthorpe, Norfolk

SIR – Major General Cowan believes that people should not sit next to their spouse at dinner. Finding myself next to my wife at a dinner party I found it necessary to discuss the dog's flatulence in the absence of the hound who was completely innocent at home.

Paul Atkins
St Albans, Hertfordshire

SIR – My wife and I enjoy sitting together when we go out to dinner. It is the only time we get to talk to each other.

Brigadier John Hemsley
Compton Martin, Somerset

FRIED FARTS FOR DINNER

SIR – My maternal grandfather's reply to any query about the next meal was: 'Pimple pamples and fried farts.' (Sorry to lower the tone.)

Phil Hunwick
Hoddlesden, Lancashire

SIR – Back in my school days, in the dinner queue on a Friday, we asked our Religious Education teacher what was for dinner and he replied, 'The piece of cod which passeth all understanding.'

Michael Stevens
Epsom, Surrey

SIR – Coming from an old Sussex family, when as a child I ever asked, 'What's for dinner?' the stock answer was always: 'Lottie dossits and plum doodies, fried fritters and buttered haycocks, knobs of chairs and pump handles, washed down with a rasher of wind and a fried snowball.'

Myrtle Paterson
Watford, Hertfordshire

SIR – My family doesn't need telling what's for dinner, as they know it's ready when the smoke alarm goes off.

William Mills
Coolham, West Sussex

SIR – Judging from recent correspondence, it seems to me that the parents of *Telegraph* readers are, for some reason, unable to answer the straightforward query, 'What's for dinner?' without resorting to whimsy or gibberish ('Flim flam, a poke in the eye and two laps of Mount Everest' or some such nonsense). Perhaps these are the same people who write the much-derided modern restaurant menu descriptions?

Matthew Lumb
Sheffield

SIR – I have just been offered 'baked beans on a bed of toast'. Is this a new low or new high?

Martyn Thomas
London SE27

SIR — The latest culinary affectation is an 'air', as in 'clementine air'. Walking in any garden one will find little patches of 'air', known as cuckoo spit, on many plants. Most of them contain the small larva of a froghopper. Not particularly attractive to eat.

Shirley Farnsworth
Hampton Hill, Middlesex

SIR — I agree with your correspondent who advocates scattering the ashes of the bereaved in the garden. My mother spent years nurturing a vine which produced no fruit. When she died her ashes were scattered around the base of the vine, and remarkably enough grapes were picked to make five bottles of white wine.

P.E.
Greywell, Hampshire

SIR — Your correspondent is understandably distressed that the neighbour's cat eats baby robins every year. Sadly, fledglings are part of a food chain. So is the cat. Eat it.

John Stringer
Harbury, Warwickshire

SIR — I suspect that most people become vegetarians not so much out of a love for animals as a hatred for plants.

Robert Readman
Bournemouth, Dorset

HAIFA HALAL

SIR — Recent correspondence regarding ritual slaughter has reminded me of an occasion in early 1947 in a residential street in Haifa. I was passing a large home with a small lawn in front, when looking over the low wall, I noticed a man, dressed similarly to a chef, holding a meat cleaver.

Running round the lawn was a headless chicken, with a small fountain of blood spurting from its neck. I will never forget his lap of honour.

Tony Pantling
Leighton Buzzard, Bedfordshire

THERE ARE MANY WAYS TO KILL A SNAIL . . .

SIR — I would like to add to the debate about which is best for luring slugs and snails to their doom: cat food or beer. I suggest both in tandem: the cat food as the lure and the beer to console the gardener when the cat food proves useless.

Bruce Denness
Whitwell, Isle of Wight

SIR — A friend of mine said she never killed snails; she threw them onto the grass verge the other side of the lane and if they were run over on the way back to her garden she considered they had committed suicide.

Dolly Langton
Warfield, Berkshire

SIR — Now that my throwing of unwanted garden snails has been curtailed by arthritis, I am considering making a scaled-down medieval trebuchet. Searching in our barn for suitable materials I came across an old clay pigeon trap. Trials last evening, witnessed by my dog, have proved most effective, with considerable distances achieved.

This method may not be practical for town dwellers. So for those living on the South Coast, could I suggest putting unwanted English snails in strawberry punnets attached to balloons? A brisk prevailing wind should achieve a speedy Channel crossing, possibly sparking off competitive snail flying races and, at the same time, feeding any itinerant hungry Frenchman.

Paul Spencer Schofield
Harewood, West Yorkshire

SIR — Yesterday, while in my garden, I lined up 10 snails on an area of rough paving and then spent at least 30 minutes watching them head off, very slowly. They showed no sense of direction, just grim determination to get elsewhere.

I thoroughly enjoyed this silent spectator sport — with no commentary.

Elizabeth French (aged 73¾)
Stoke St Mary, Somerset

SIR — I have found that by polishing one side of the snail and coming in off a shortened run across my balcony, I can swing the snail around the large apple tree at the bottom of my garden and safely into my neighbour's garden beyond.

Scott Clapworthy
Shrewsbury

SPORTING TRIUMPH AND DISASTER

ENGLAND'S REPUTATION BURNT TO ASHES

SIR — I am in the course of reading what has become my eagerly awaited and most cherished Christmas present, *The Daily Telegraph's* book of unpublished letters.

All was going well until the section headed: 'Australia's Reputation Burnt to Ashes'. In future, should England ever recover from an Ashes series where they have been bemused, bewildered, hobbled and cobbled, could you please refrain from printing correspondents' letters containing such insights as, 'This is no good. Michael Clarke is too nice', and 'the widespread decline in Australian sporting success is remarkable', in order not to provide the Aussies with such effective motivational material.

You may wish to investigate if anyone provided the Aussies with a leaked advance copy of *Am I Missing Something . . .?*

Mike Haberfield
Springfield, Buckinghamshire

SIR — Yesterday a letter arrived on my doorstep from my aunt Olive, born, bred and resident in Australia. I opened it with considerable trepidation because I knew all too well what it would contain:

'The Sydney Test was simply embarrassing — I

like a close game. Apart from the plain facts that our bowling and batting were much better, I'll make these comments. Cook, while seemingly a nice man, was a hopeless leader. He was no tactician, his management of fielders was inept, and on the field he was passive . . .

'The English fielding was awful. When I played baseball and cricket all those years ago, we were taught how to field and catch. The English disobeyed all the rules as I know them . . .

'Pietersen played flamboyantly when he should have been digging in. Swann departed suddenly with a very unpleasant parting shot at his fellow players. Anderson's bowling was innocuous . . .'

Olive is well into her 93rd year. When one of its most senior citizens can produce an analysis as cogent as anything outside the pages of *Wisden*, it seems little wonder that Australia's cricketers have recently annihilated ours.

Michael Raw
Sedbergh, Cumbria

SIR — Since the England women's team have just won the Ashes, the answer to England's woeful men's cricket fortunes seems obvious.

John Moore
London W7

SIR – A popular family expression in our household for ineptitude was, 'You are about as useful as a chocolate teapot.'

I now suggest: 'You are about as useful as a fifth day Ashes Test Match ticket.'

Graham Dixon
Hornby, Lancashire

SIR – I understand that 235 years ago a certain Captain Cook was overcome and eaten up by the hostile locals in the Pacific.

Craig Kennedy
Brookfield, Renfrewshire

SIR – When we invited England to send an Ashes team to Australia we didn't mean the remains of 11 former cricketers.

David Samuel
Richmond, New South Wales, Australia

SIR – As a colonial I am a little ignorant of the honours system and hope you may enlighten me. Does OBE stand for Ordinary Bowling Effort or Ordinary Batting Effort? Either way, I think Her Majesty should most certainly be handing out some more of them to your English cricket team.

Stephen Driscoll
Carlingford, New South Wales, Australia

SIR – As a visitor to Sydney the worst part of the humiliating Ashes defeat is that the Australian media is asking its readers and listeners to be gentle and kind to Englishmen and to buy a Pom a beer. I far preferred it when we were whingers.

James Osborne
Canterbury, Kent

SIR – Just when it appears that matters cannot get any worse, we are subject to the England captain telling us in the post-match press conference that 'only Broads and Stokesie came out of the series with any credit'.

I despair. Somebody should remind 'Cookie' that he is in charge of the national team, not the local pub team, and that in the current circumstances a little decorum is required.

Neil Parsons
Laceby, Lincolnshire

SIR – Steven Gerrard for England cricket captain?

Michele Platman
Birmingham

SIR – Several things are beginning to seriously annoy me with cricket on television: close-ups of Alastair Cook picking his nose and inspecting the result; several players spitting; and the overdone high fiving, hand clapping, hugging and general euphoria at every wicket fall.

I find this 'modern' approach totally repugnant and unsporting.

Jack Phillip
Dedham, Essex

SIR – I am about to write a book about England's cricket team entitled, *How to Lose a Cricket Match*. I anticipate it will run to about 300 pages.

Dr David Gutmann
London N12

SIR – Britain's standards have fallen to a new low this week with the legalisation of same-sex marriage, being beaten at cricket by the Netherlands and the *Telegraph* describing the late Professor Margaret Spufford as 'a historian'. Is there no hope for us?

Hugh Linnell
Leiston, Suffolk

PIETERSEN'S FINAL DISMISSAL

SIR – As a follower of England cricket for many decades, I am disappointed we will not be seeing Kevin Pietersen bat for England again.

I watched him score 71 at Melbourne on Boxing Day and from start to finish it was enthralling. He was lucky not to be out early when a fielder stepped over the boundary rope after catching a hook shot; he cross-batted Mitchell Johnston through mid on for four while apparently troubled by injury; and he was out to what an Australian newspaper described as 'the biggest, most ambitious and agricultural heave ever aimed at a ball by a recognised batsman'.

It was fantastic entertainment. I will miss it.

Barry Smith
Loughborough, Leicestershire

SIR – The slogging game masquerading as 20-over cricket can be improved. Make hitting the ball straight over the boundary an instant dismissal.

George Noon
Fulwood, Lancashire

SIR – Pietersen is the classic old-fashioned man. He is the hero who would be sent out to face the enemy in single combat. He is the hunter who would have returned with meat in the coldest winter. He is not a symptom of a new world, rather an anachronism from an old world where people lived or died depending on the success of their warriors and hunters.

Nowadays technology means that none of us in the developed world risk starvation. Corporations are too big to fail, and when they do, they are bailed out by a compliant government. We no longer believe we need heroes. It's all about team players who never rock the boat or rage against the machine.

Amazingly, now that we have purged our banks, our public service and our sporting teams of anyone who is not a yes-man, we have less success than ever before.

Kevin Pietersen's weakness was not that he picked on the weak, it was that he stood up to the strong. It is people like him that bring us all forward. They carry the weaker members of society and turn all their righteous rage on the strong.

I know from experience what happens to organisations that crush the voice of dissent. They fail.

Roger Sweetman
Galway, Ireland

SIR — To those fretting over Kevin Pietersen's dismissal, surely the fact that the likes of Piers Morgan, Shane Warne and Michael Vaughan are in his corner is incontrovertible evidence that, for once, the ECB has made the right decision.

David Hallowell
Tadworth, Surrey

SIR — I often struggle to read all the articles in your Sport section so I am grateful to you for hiring Kevin Pietersen. There will be at least two pages I will be able to omit.

Why have you done it?

Michael Harding
Chalfont St Peter, Buckinghamshire

LIES AND DAMNED LIES

SIR — You report the formula of William Hartston, a Cambridge mathematician, for picking the Grand National winner. I have a similar formula: statistically, nobody wearing a mauve sock on their left hand and a yellow one on their right foot has ever been involved in a plane crash.

Graham Chapman
London SE3

SCHUMACHER'S SKIING

SIR – At an induction course at Farnborough in 1957 I was shown a fighter pilot's helmet. The pilot had to eject from his plane at take off. It was too low for his parachute to deploy properly but this was his only chance. He separated from his ejected seat, landed on his head and skidded thereon for some 20 yards. He survived.

The helmet was structurally intact apart from a small crack in one layer on X-ray, and a slight fraying of one strap.

If such technology was available more than 50 years ago how is it that Schumacher's helmet broke in half upon impact with a rock?

Dr Alan D. Prowse
Leatherhead, Surrey

SIR – I am very happy to learn that Michael Schumacher is out of his coma and that he has been able to return to Switzerland after almost six months in hospital in France.

Monsieur L'Inspecteur des impôts, ever mindful of France's parlous economic state, must have had his beady eye on this particular canard, sitting or otherwise, that has now been able to flap to a more congenial nest.

Sir Victor Walker, Bt
St Antonin du Var, Provence-Alpes-Côte d'Azur, France

THE UGLY GAME

SIR – Why do they call football 'the Beautiful Game'? As far as I can see it consists of two gangs of thugs charging up and down a field, spitting profusely, screaming insults at the referee and generally attempting to maim each other.

True, a ball seems to figure somewhere, but only to pass the time between the aforementioned activities.

Barbara Whalley
Nantwich, Cheshire

SIR – Have World Cup referees noticed that footballers spend 90 minutes pretending they're injured, and rugby players spend 80 minutes pretending they're not?

The laws of physics appear to be reversed, in that rugby players are impossible to knock over, yet footballers go down if someone coughs.

Philip Saunders
Ditchingham, Suffolk

SIR – Is display of pain somehow related in reverse proportion to income? Why do footballers writhe about as if hit by a magazine of high-velocity rounds after the most cursory contact with another player, whereas jump jockeys get up after falling on to similar turf, from a height of up to 12 feet, travelling at near on 30mph?

Nicky Samengo-Turner
Hundon, Suffolk

SIR – I am a rugby man but inevitably I have been watching the World Cup. In my opinion, football needs more excitement, by which I mean goals. In particular, I understand the all-important American audience needs more action.

I suggest that the size of the goalmouth is increased by the average increase in height of a Premier League goalkeeper when the laws of football were written and the average height of a goalkeeper today.

One further thought: can one imagine how exciting extra time would be if it were played after the penalty shootout? The 'losing' team going hell for leather to score would make for compelling action.

I do not wish for Sepp Blatter's job, just some of his perks.

Keith Shannon
Bungay, Suffolk

SIR — Sepp Blatter simply can't have grasped the basics of corruption if he's still having to work full-time at the age of 78.

Cynthia Harrod-Eagles
Northwood, Middlesex

SIR — Having been a football fan for as long as I can remember, I now wonder if children should be banned from watching the game as it has altered beyond recognition.

The players sport hideous haircuts and some have to wear Alice bands to keep their hair out of their eyes. They wear a pair of their granny's knickers under their shorts and have begun to wear pretty coloured shoes; at the World Cup some cannot even get a matching pair. Goalkeepers have the same problem with their gloves.

If they are fortunate enough to score a goal they run around with their mouths wide open like a wild animal, hands and face turned toward the heavens, until their teammates catch them, piling on top until they have all given each other a kiss. Nowadays the coaching staff also join in.

If a decision goes against them they mob the referee, while their manager tackles the fourth official. If the team wins they dance up and down like little girls waiting for the lavatory. If they lose, many cry.

For years players have exchanged shirts with the opposition. Last week some even exchanged shorts. What next?

The lunatics really have taken over the asylum.

John N. Gibson
Kirkburton, West Yorkshire

SIR – Having seen the exhibition which players make of themselves, I wonder whether men are becoming more like women used to be.

Geoffrey Geere
Abingdon, Oxfordshire

SIR – I am aware that there is a Golden Boot award for the top goal scorer in the World Cup, but wondered if there is also a prize for the nuttiest hairstyle worn by a footballer? There are certainly plenty from which to choose.

John R.M. Prime
Old Bedhampton, Hampshire

SIR – In these days of minute and expensive analysis of sportspeople's diet, psychological state, fitness regime, running style diagnostics, and so on, should not the hairstyles of footballers – namely those containing gel, asymmetrical partings, shaved areas and braids – be assessed with regards to their efficiency and accuracy while heading the ball?

Just looking at the bewildering number of different styles sported by the French World Cup team alone would keep a team of boffins frantically tapping at their laptops for weeks.

Belinda Jones
London SW17

ENGLAND'S USELESS TOFFS

SIR — Perhaps the most remarkable statistic from the World Cup is that former independent school pupils were twice as likely to be selected for the England squad as former state school pupils.

Independent schools, which educate seven per cent of the country, produced three of the 23 squad members (0.429 for each one per cent from that sector), whereas the state sector produced 20 (0.215 for each one per cent from the sector).

It makes the 70 per cent greater chance of gaining a place at Cambridge for independent school applicants look like a poor showing.

Malcolm Warburton
Sandbach, Cheshire

SIR — Following the recent embarrassing performances of our national football and cricket teams, is there any way we could swap the sports over, thus playing Sri Lanka at football, and Uruguay and Italy at cricket?

Bob McCallum
Waltham St Lawrence, Berkshire

SIR — The punishment for failure at the World Cup? Wayne Rooney having to carry his own bag to the Bentley waiting to take him home.

James Little
Ropley, Hampshire

SIR — After seeing photos of England's sad and scruffy football failures slinking home yesterday it occurred to me that perhaps our problem is that these poor young chaps simply aren't paid enough. You may recall this approach worked rather well with our excellent bankers.

Phil Mason
Tunbridge Wells, Kent

SIR — Your sports pundits wrote today that Rooney should play in his preferred position and that Ashley Cole should have been in the English squad. Both of these opinions were expressed frequently by my husband before they left the country, not in hindsight.

Pauline Davies
Silverton, Devon

SIR – I simply do not understand why my husband was not chosen for one of the teams competing in the World Cup. Or even to referee. Our home commentary is far from dull.

Gay Fearn
Haywards Heath, West Sussex

SIR – How long before we come to accept that 1966 was the worst year ever for English football? It fed us a lifetime's delusion that we have a world-class side.

Ted Wilson
Hucclecote, Gloucestershire

SIR – After the England World Cup fiasco the answer is to make their nemesis, Luis Suarez, the next manager. That job should really give him something to get his teeth into.

Geoff Milburn
Glossop, Derbyshire

SIR – If FIFA clears Luis Suarez of all wrongdoing can we expect that, should Uruguay play Germany at some stage during the World Cup, he will be allowed two bites of the Jerry?

Robin Peters
Bath

A FALLIBLE FINAL

SIR – I predict an unholy atmosphere at the Vatican on Sunday with the Argentine Pope supporting one side and his German predecessor the other.

Dominic Shelmerdine
London SW3

SIR – So the World Cup final is between Germany and Argentina: the country that gave birth to the Nazis versus the country that sheltered them.

Robert Readman
Bournemouth, Dorset

SIR – It appears the best way to get into a World Cup final is to have picked a fight with the British at some time in the past.

Jonathan L. Kelly
Yatton, Somerset

SIR – Looking at your double-page photograph
of the German World Cup squad, it would seem
that a cosmetic dentist is also part of their winning
entourage.

Fran Pater
Whitstable, Kent

SIR – Germany deserved to win the World Cup.
They had the fewest daft haircuts and tattoos.

J.M.
Casterton, Cumbria

SIR – The Germans may have won the World
Cup but the Brazilians have much sexier looking
women.

Ted Shorter
Hildenborough, Kent

SIR – After the seventh goal was scored in the
Germany versus Brazil semi-final, should not the
referee have asked for new balls?

B. Potter
Finchampstead, Berkshire

EXCLUSIVE WIMBLEDON CONUNDRUMS

SIR – Watching Wimbledon doubles tennis I feel increasingly excluded. There are secret hand signals from the server's partner; whispered tactics behind cupped hands; and the annoying bonding after every point (or are notes being exchanged?).

What is going on? Perhaps 'hawk-ear' could be introduced?

Patrick Chillery
Fishbourne, West Sussex

SIR – Tennis players used to blow on their nails. Why? And why have they stopped?

Philip Hobson
Great Stukeley, Cambridgeshire

SIR – A couple of years ago it was de rigueur for all players to consume many bananas during a Wimbledon match. This year I have noticed only a couple being consumed. What does the tennis fraternity know about bananas that we don't?

Alan Belk
Leatherhead, Surrey

SIR — I have recently returned from a cruise for which I was able to take as much luggage as I could physically manage. My case for 12 days was smaller than any of the bags carried on court for a match lasting four hours. What, I wonder, is in the inner depths of these bags?

David Miller
Tickhill, South Yorkshire

SIR — One of the most annoying and seemingly pointless aspects of Wimbledon is the slow handclap by the crowd each time a review is called to see whether the ball was in or out.

Why? Have I missed something?

John Gray
Kelsall, Cheshire

SIR — Can anyone tell me how groups of Australian tennis supporters manage to acquire at least six or more seats together?

L.H.
Bristol

SIR — Was that a cardboard cut-out of Victoria Beckham in the crowd? Surely nobody could be so impassive? Perhaps the seat could be given to an interested person next time.

Roger K. Bentley
Chorley, Lancashire

SIR — Not being in the same room as the television, but well within earshot, I was unsure if I was listening to Wimbledon or *Casualty*.

John Townshend
South Wootton, Norfolk

SIR — The grunters in the game pale into insignificance compared to Rafael Nadal's wardrobe adjustments.

My concern stems from the fact that, at the age of eight, I was dispatched to a noted boarding school and, in my innocence and the absence of anything else, wore baggy boxer shorts. These gave me similar problems to those seemingly displayed by Mr Nadal. Chafing and complications from fallout (even at that tender age) resulted in frequent adjustments being required — much to the amusement of my merciless contemporaries.

I eventually gained the experience (and the funds)

to address the problem and, through my teenage years, invested in Y-fronts. These proved a remarkable improvement to my former state but did not totally solve the problem: in certain amorous experiences, Y-fronts did not prevent fallout either.

I moved on to elasticated boxer shorts which proved a miracle. Everything seemed to stay where it should and I have spent the last 40 years well contented in this department.

I would gladly offer Mr Nadal the benefit of my experience. Otherwise, could we possibly ask the BBC to shoot him from the waist upwards for the remainder of the tournament?

T.C.
Bristol

SIR – After the latest edict from the Lawn Tennis Association on women wearing all-white knickers, I would like to volunteer as a checker.

Joking apart, the white rule is very easy to enforce: I have yet to see a ladies match where their underwear wasn't exposed.

Simon Palmer
Portland, Dorset

SIR – The women tennis players at Wimbledon seem to become prettier by the year. I am 75 and, *Deo volente*, eagerly look forward to my eighties.

Robert Fromow
London SW1

THE LAST BRITISH WINNER FOR 77 YEARS

SIR – Halfway through the second week of Wimbledon and not a mention of the name Fred Perry. I only hope that, should I have grandchildren, they aren't sitting here in 70-odd years listening to some commentator saying, 'Not since Andrew Murray in 2013 . . .'

Phil Warner
Alvechurch, Worcestershire

SIR – There is one positive to be taken from Andy Murray being out of Wimbledon. At least we will not have to put up with childish antics from Alex Salmond.

Brian Earle
Birnie, Morayshire

SIR – Presumably if Scotland vote for independence, we will all have to go back to idolising Fred Perry.

Mick Ferrie
Mawnan Smith, Cornwall

SIR – I've just seen Andy Murray talking about his 'confidence'. What is it with 'confidence issues' nonsense these days? Everyone from celebrities to *X Factor* contestants seems to suffer from the affliction. Last year it was depression, this year this.

When I was a ward manager I didn't stand outside the ward doors wringing my hands about my confidence. Nor when I became a nursing lecturer. I just got on with it, like everyone does.

Too much psychobabble in modern society.

R.K.
Leeds

TOUR D'ILKLEY

SIR – I come from an age when cycling was an ordinary form of transport used by ordinary folk. No special clothing was required, apart, perhaps, from cycle clips, required to stop one's trouser-cuffs getting oily.

Nowadays nobody seems to be able to cycle

anywhere without dressing up like a full-blown racer.

Well, I tell you, sir, it's getting out of hand. I nipped in to Ilkley for a pint at lunchtime, and there were hundreds of the blighters, all dressed up to the nines like they were in the Tour de France or something. Madness!

Christopher Monniot
Rodley, West Yorkshire

SIR – Yorkshire embraced the Tour de France with magnificence: good hospitality, a friendly atmosphere, beautiful scenery, yellow bikes and sheep, and roads lined with supporters.

Cambridge, meanwhile, complained because one road is going to be closed for a few hours.

Does this prove once and for all that Northerners are much more friendly?

Janice Moss
Altrincham, Cheshire

SIR – As a proud Yorkshire man, who moved to the wrong side of the Pennines (as a missionary) some 30 years ago, I was delighted to be reminded of what I am missing during the broadcasts of the 'Grand Depart' over the weekend. I'm sure the pictures relayed across the globe will entice visitors to God's own County over the coming years.

However, I was taken aback by all the comments expressing surprise that hundreds of thousands of fellow Yorkshire folk had turned out to support the Tour de France. Such numbers were obviously to be expected at the event: it was free.

John Ross
Crewe, Cheshire

SIR – I was particularly struck by the commentators' inadequacy when an enterprising couple were seen doing a very creditable, and obviously well-rehearsed, can-can routine on a grass verge outside Ripon as the peloton passed.

The numpty (good Yorkshire word) commentator referred to the two as doing 'some sort of Yorkshire jig there'.

Lindsay Addyman
Great Ouseburn, North Yorkshire

SIR – The biggest surprise of the English stage of the Tour was that no cyclists were seen on the pavements.

Guy Rose
London SW14

A LUDICROUS SPORTING YEAR

SIR – The Ashes, Brazil, Headingly, Wimbledon, Le Tour: could one of your classically educated readers give me the Latin for sporting washout? *Annus horribilis ludus* perhaps? Or perhaps just *ludicrous*?

Mike Morris
Old Swinford, West Midlands

A LUDICROUS PASTIME

SIR – Who was the misguided fool who invented the ball? Did he/she (surely not?) not realise that future generations would have to suffer football, tennis, golf, snooker – the list is almost endless? Television schedules are worthless and loving families are rent asunder.

Mrs J.M. Sharp
Alfrick, Worcestershire

SIR – We all have pet annoyances, things that irritate, distract and puzzle, but in the great scheme of things do not add up to a hill of beans.

Mine is television showing crowd scenes on the big screen at sporting events. Broadcasters are determined that everyone should continually watch the screen rather than the pitch, and then when they catch sight of themselves they must behave like children — even during the anthems.

This rather perfectly reflects Jeremy Paxman's insistence that 13-year-olds are now in charge of everything in the media.

Huw Beynon
Llandeilo, Carmarthenshire

DUKE AND DUCHESS OF JONAH

SIR — David Cameron has often been accused of being a Jonah, but is it not time to keep Kate and Wills away from any sporting event involving British competitors?

First the England football team saw their hopes dashed at the World Cup after a good luck message from Prince William. Then Andy Murray lost form and fell from grace, witnessed by William and a gurning Kate. Then the couple looked on as Mark Cavendish literally crashed out of the Tour de France under their ill-starred gaze.

I can only recommend white heather and a rabbit's foot to anyone spying the Duke and Duchess of Cambridge in the crowd.

Anthony Rodriguez
Staines Upon Thames, Middlesex

ROYAL FLUSHES

ROYAL SUN ALLIANCE

SIR – Many congratulations to Prince Philip on his 93rd birthday. I see he is going to Germany on Thursday. Where does he get his travel insurance?

Brian Baxter
Oakington, Cambridgeshire

SIR – With a choice of almost any gem in the world, has anyone noticed that Her Majesty wears the same pearl earrings in every photo taken of her? Perhaps she would like to send the ones she doesn't wear to me?

Val Hiscock
Llandrindod, Powys

SIR – The Queen should be commended for sharing her workload with Prince Charles. If David Cameron wants a break I am quite willing to fill in for him.

Eddie Peart
Rotherham, South Yorkshire

THE PRINCE AND THE PUTIN

SIR – My grandson, a pupil aged 14 at Monmouth School, has recently completed a history project of his own choice, in which he compared Hitler with Putin. How should it be marked and should he send it to Prince Charles?

> **Dr Jeremy Telling**
> Abbots Leigh, Somerset

SIR – Prince Charles compares Vladimir Putin with Hitler. I suggest a more apposite comparison would be with Al Capone.

> **Sandy Pratt**
> Dormansland, Surrey

SIR – Vladimir Putin says that these comments are not worthy of a monarch. How would he know? His country murdered their monarchs.

> **Nigel Parsons**
> Cardiff

SIR – Has anyone asked President Putin what he thinks of Prince Charles?

> **Dr John Doherty**
> Vienna, Austria

SIR – How many of your readers are surprised that Labour spokesmen seem to have been much more vocal criticising Prince Charles than over the whole Ukrainian crisis?

Neville Seabridge
Thoroton, Nottinghamshire

WHERE DID PRINCE CHARLES GO TO SCHOOL?

SIR – While watching the Prince of Wales touring the Somerset levels I spotted the tie he was wearing. For the life of me I cannot remember him attending Consett Grammar, but then he must have been four forms above me.

David Laybourne
Ilfracombe, Devon

SIR – From the photographs HRH's tie looks very much like the Walsall Golf Club tie. But I very much doubt that it is.

P.J. Wheatley
Hadley, Shropshire

SIR — I bet he is looking forward to the day he retires and, like me, can throw all his ties in the bin.

Mike Jones
Botwnnog, Gwynedd

FARMER WILLS

SIR — Apparently Prince William is going on a ten-week agricultural course. How much will he learn in that time, I wonder? When I was called up to do my National Service, it took eight weeks to learn how to march.

Peter McPherson
Merriott, Somerset

SIR — The Duke of Cambridge's short university farming course reminds me of Ringo Starr's answer when asked if he had hands-on experience of gardening on his estate. 'Well, I do a lot of pointing,' he replied.

Kevin Platt
Walsall, West Midlands

OUR MAN IN THE ANTIPODES

SIR – Now is the time to send Prince Harry to the Antipodes to prove that we can be just as mental as they are, thus preserving the Commonwealth.

David Alsop
Churchdown, Gloucestershire

SIR – When I was a young officer casting around for a woman I cast wide. To judge from your photograph on page one, Cressida Bonas, Prince Harry's ex-girlfriend, should know I'm glad I found one who could do up her shoelaces.

Dr Michael Downing
Allesley, West Midlands

HOLD THE FRONT PAGE

SIR – Although her countenance has already graced your pages several times in recent days, am I alone in predicting that the one racing certainty of Royal Ascot week is that yet another large photograph of the Duchess of Cambridge, or her mother or sister, will soon appear on your pages?

The only uncertainty is on which day and page. My money's on Friday's front page. Am I right?

John Hewitson
Puttenham, Surrey

SIR — Today we learn that Pippa Middleton's 'fondness for table tennis is well documented'. If that is so do we really need to have a whole page devoted to her?

Even my husband wonders why we need to see her on such a regular basis.

Yvonne Carse
Launceston, Cornwall

SIR — If I see another feature starring Pippa Middleton I shall probably turn to drink.

C.R.
Thruxton, Hampshire

SIR — Can I have a job as a superficial columnist please, just like Pippa Middleton?

Jeremy Bloomfield
East Stour, Dorset

SIR – While I would be the first to admit that Pippa looked wonderful in black lycra, any regular cyclist will strongly advise against wearing black top and bottoms as it renders you almost invisible to other road users.

Graham Ricketts
St Albans, Hertfordshire

SIR – If just about everyone in a room is wearing a 'high-vis' jacket, as per your photograph on page four today, then surely each loses their conspicuousness?

Sam Kelly
Dobcross, West Yorkshire

ANTI-SOCIAL
MEDIA

ANTI-SOCIAL TWITS

SIR – I constantly read references to websites such as Facebook and Twitter as 'Social Media'. To watch, as I regularly do, four or five people sitting round a table all busy tapping away with their handheld devices indicates the opposite.

Michael Orpen-Palmer
Hove, East Sussex

SIR – On the odd occasion that I have ventured into a Costafairbuck to enjoy a quiet coffee I am assailed by loud piped 'music' and the occasional sound of a pig being slaughtered in the vicinity. Conversation is impossible and bliss it is to return to the comparative quiet of the high street.

D.B.
Lavenham, Suffolk

SIR – There seems to be a new pandemic affecting millions of people: Intercontinental Verbal Incontinence Syndrome makes the sufferers believe that they ought to communicate with unknown individuals across the globe regarding the most trivial topics.

Surely the pharmaceutical companies could produce a brain-numbing drug to relieve them from the urge to constantly tap the keys on their smart phones?

Anand Deshpande
Westhoughton, Lancashire

SIR – How about making it a criminal offence to use a mobile phone in the presence of a child?

Elizabeth Ramsbottom
Lichfield, Staffordshire

SIR – From my experience, going online is akin to watching very early black and white silent movies. Is this the best modern technology can produce?

E.F.
Durham

SIR – As a simple soul, baffled by modern technology, I have often wondered how it could be that human beings were clever enough to design all this stuff. The answer has now come to me in a revelatory flash: these people are not human beings at all; they are aliens sent to earth in human form to bring our technology levels up to those of their own planet so as to make our world suitable for colonisation.

Bruce Nicolls
Portsmouth

THE CHELSEA PRESENTERS' SHOW

SIR – Sophie Raworth tells us she has a garden.
Gosh. Yes, it's The Chelsea Presenters Show again.
If only flowers could talk, we might see a bit more of
them and know their names.

Amanda Mansell
Lavenham, Suffolk

SIR – The 'h' in the RHS Chelsea Flower Show
suggests horticulture, but watching the BBC
television coverage makes me wonder if it should be
organised by the Royal Design Society.

Several uses of the word zeitgeist (*Gott im Himmel!*)
earlier in the week rather confirmed this.

Michael Fielding
Winchester, Hampshire

SIR – It seems that all flowers have to be white or
blue or not there at all. Sad.

Edward Hawkins
Shipbourne, Kent

SIR – Now that memory of another Chelsea
Flower Show fades, my wife and I still remember
the enjoyment of watching TV interviewers while
the sound was switched off. Their gesticulations

resembled those of band conductors minus their batons. Is it possible for professional speakers to talk without frantically waving their hands about?

Robert Vincent
Wildhern, Hampshire

EUROVISION BEARD CONTEST

SIR – In future Eurovision Song Contests, to avoid political voting and expensive razzmatazz, I think the female singer with the best beard should be declared the winner.

Nairn Lawson
Portbury, Somerset

SIR – Am I alone in thinking that the winner of this year's Eurovision Song Contest was also its Wurst?

Andrew H.N. Gray
Edinburgh

SIR – The Eurovision winner has a striking name as well as a striking appearance. *Conchita* is Spanish slang for 'vagina' and *Wurst* is German for 'sausage'.

Andy Bugden
Shenzhen, Guangdong, China

SIR – Having endured the Eurovision Song
Contest, any remaining doubts I might have had
about voting UKIP have now been dispelled.

Allan Kirtley
Valley End, Surrey

SIR – Britain's standing in Europe now appears
directly related to its position in the contest.

Ainslie Bazely
Sanderstead, Surrey

SIR – Are we all missing the point regarding
devolution for Scotland? If it means they have their
own entry in The Eurovision Song Contest, they
could vote for our entry – and we could vote for
theirs.

Jon Stride
Sherborne, Dorset

SIR – I propose that the voting system for the
European Parliament be changed to the one used
in the Eurovision Song Contest. Each voter would
assign 0 to 12 points to candidates in foreign
countries. This would reflect the detachment that
most people feel from the European Parliament.

While the votes are counted, there could be a
subsidiary contest in which each nation puts up one

of their candidates to make a three-minute speech in whichever language they choose.

It would be more interesting than what we have now.

Michael Gorman
Guildford, Surrey

SIR – That the nations of Europe should vote for such a travesty of entertainment really does beggar belief.

On a day when the *Telegraph* published a photograph of the might of the Russian fleet sailing up the English Channel, accompanied by a lone Royal Navy destroyer, we should be thinking of re-building our navy and armed forces, not frittering away capital on Europe.

Perhaps Mr Putin would consider becoming our MEP for the north-west of England. If he did, he would certainly get my vote, particularly after the splendour of the Moscow Victory Parade.

Major Graham Dixon (retd)
Lancaster

COULSON FOR BRUSSELS

SIR – The recent court decision in the *News of the World* case offers the Prime Minister a solution for a job vacancy. He should follow Tony Blair's example when he appointed Peter Mandelson and put up Andy Coulson as UK Commissioner to the EU.

John Letchford
Elsenham, Hertfordshire

SIR – You report that Andy Coulson had not been told that phone hacking is illegal. Perhaps someone should tell him that murder, theft and going through a red light are also illegal before he gets into further trouble.

Ken Himsworth
Saxilby, Lincolnshire

SIR – Proof, finally, that women cannot multitask. Rebekah Brooks was able to run a company but was unable to spot what was going on. I can die happy.

Jonathan Fulford
Bosham, West Sussex

SIR — If I am ever accused of anything, please may I have the same jury as Rebekah Brooks?

Chris Doe
Broad Campden, Gloucestershire

SIR — Now that the waiting is over for Rebekah Brooks and she has been found not guilty of phone hacking will she get a haircut?

J.S. Huggins
Mylor Harbour, Cornwall

SIR — Am I alone in finding it odd that the state spends tens of millions prosecuting people for listening to the telephone messages of a few minor celebrities, while GCHQ, a branch of the state, listens to and records the telephone calls of all of us?

Charles Pugh
London SW10

SIR — Should MI5 wish to review my email traffic and my phone calls they are welcome, if they can withstand the mundane conversations. In doing so, perhaps they can find where I left my mobile phone; if it helps, I know it is somewhere in my home, probably alongside the last one I lost.

Alan Belk
Leatherhead, Surrey

SIR – I have always thought that I knew how the protest group Hacked Off got its name. In the light of recent revelations I now realise that it's what at least three women would like to do to a small part of Hugh Grant's anatomy.

Ron Mason
East Grinstead, West Sussex

THE SUN SETS ON ROLF HARRIS

SIR – Suddenly I feel old and sad. As a teenager 50 years ago 'Sun Arise' by Rolf Harris seemed to represent not only the wonderful rich diversity of 1960s' music, but also my own growing familiarity with a working life.

Now the sun has set on that, along with any regard for Mr Harris.

Phillip Crossland
Nafferton, East Yorkshire

SIR – Rolf Harris has been sentenced according to the laws when the crimes were committed. When shall we expect the next hanging?

Michael Ware
Cardiff

SIR — Reading the content of the letter allegedly
written by Rolf Harris and read to the jury at his trial
I was reminded of my late father, who was a solicitor
for 50 years. He gave me two pieces of advice: 'Marry
for love, but if she has money so much the better';
and 'Never, ever, write a letter without wondering
how it would sound if read out in Court.'

Jeremy Gibbons QC
Mannington, Dorset

SIR — I note on television that every time Rolf
Harris attends Southwark Court, there is a huge
Marks & Spencer lorry in the background. How
do they manage this with London's draconian
parking regulations? Do they supply the court with
sandwiches?

John Buggins
Sutton Coldfield, West Midlands

SIR — The Roman civilisation came to an end in
a sea of corruption and sexual depravity. In the
light of the revelations about endemic sexual abuse
and corruption are we about to see the end of our
current era?

Duncan Rayner
Sunningdale, Berkshire

SIR – Both Melita Norwood, the KGB spy, and Rolf Harris were exposed in their early eighties as wicked people. Harris, quite rightly, has felt the full force of the law. Unfairly, Letty, as she was known during her childhood friendship with my Aunt Blanche, was spared police action.

On the other hand, Harris did not have to suffer the ignominy of being crossed off my aunt's Christmas card list.

Rosemary Earle
Swindon, Wiltshire

PHILIP SEYMOUR WHO?

SIR – A great fuss is being made about the death of Philip Seymour Hoffman. I cannot find anybody who has ever heard of him.

Michael Watts
Penrith, Cumbria

BRAZILIAN STREET

SIR – Am I the only one to be put off by the *Coronation Street* barmaids constantly filing their fingernails while on duty? Surely this must conflict with food and beer sales hygiene regulations?

Perhaps they should go the whole hog and shave their arm pits or have a DIY Brazilian at the same time?

Ted Shorter
Hildenborough, Kent

THE LIFE OF BIRDS

SIR — I see that the Head of the Natural History Unit at the BBC is going to replace David Attenborough with yet another pretty girl who is going to give us wildlife programmes that are 'entertainment and fun' with talking animals. I thought we got that once from Rod Hull and Emu.

What's wrong with straightforward information and facts? Some of us do actually understand words of more than one syllable.

John Salkeld
London SE22

SIR — Having recently seen two televised documentaries featuring Darcey Bussell, I wonder if she could be the loveliest personality on the planet.

Ron Ward
Axminster, Devon

COMPLICATED, DEAR WATSON

SIR – I fail to understand the gush and fawning over *Sherlock* on BBC One. Leaving aside the trees in full leaf on Christmas Day, the plots require Holmes' skills of deduction to unpick the sledgehammer scene changes, delivered with the panache of applying make-up at sea in a hurricane.

Charles Foster
Chalfont St Peter, Buckinghamshire

SIR – I find all the eulogies concerning the new series of Sherlock Holmes baffling. It is what used to be known in Penny Dreadfuls as, 'With one bound Jack was free'.

Please let us return to the 19th century.

Adrian Holloway
Minchinhampton, Gloucestershire

SIR – I rather doubt Sherlock Holmes would set foot on the streets of London with the lowest button of his waistcoat done up, unless, of course, he wished to disguise himself as an Italian dancing master. As for the matching gloves and tie, style is not the word I would apply.

Christopher Harris
Ponteland, Northumberland

SIR — If Sherlock Holmes is so bloody clever why doesn't he know the difference between the Grenadier and Welsh Guards and why doesn't he know that in the Brigade of Guards an Other Rank is called Guardsman and not Private?

Brian Inns (formerly Grenadier Guards)
Chertsey, Surrey

SIR — Did anyone notice that in Sherlock's mental run down of Mary, Watson's girlfriend, he listed her as a *Guardian* reader?

P. Banton
Burton on Trent, Staffordshire

SIR — How sad that the brilliance of last night's production of Sherlock Holmes was strangely fractured by twice using the American pronunciation of *leverage*.

John Turner
Ely, Cambridgeshire

IT'S (NOT) GOOD TO MUMBLE

SIR — Night three of the *Jamaica Inn* BBC dramatisation was much akin to a BT call centre, without BT's sense of drama. Is there a connection between these two national institutions we should know about?

> **Philip Hodgkins**
> Grosmont, Monmouthshire

SIR — Will the next episode of *Jamaica Inn* be set in Mumbles?

> **Paul Burlinson**
> Parwich, Derbyshire

SIR — As I am deaf and had the subtitles on, I watched it blissfully unaware of its faults. It secretly gives me quite a kick to realise that in just three hours a large number of people had a small inkling of what it is like to be deaf.

> **Judith Barker**
> Hailsham, East Sussex

SIR — The BBC's so-called flagship drama flopped not only because the dialogue was mostly inaudible, but also because the action took place almost entirely in the dark and all the characters and props looked as though they needed a really good wash.

Alec O'Connor
West Horsley, Surrey

SIR – When it wasn't dark it was either very misty or pouring with rain. Those of us who go on holiday in Cornwall will have spent a few days on the beach sheltering from the elements but really, couldn't we have had a bit more of the glorious Cornish sunshine? The poor girl had been there for months and was well into the third episode before the sun came out.

Personally, I think the whole thing was a plot by the Spanish Tourist Board to boost their holiday numbers and nothing to do with technical problems at the Beeb.

Andrew Perrins
Upton on Severn, Worcestershire

SIR – The BBC's production of *Jamaica Inn* included, unusually, not one Scottish accent, so I rather enjoyed it.

Paul Downey
Cutwell, Gloucestershire

ARROWS OUT FOR *THE ARCHERS*

SIR — *The Archers* has gone off a bit. Ridiculous story lines have resulted in: Tony being permanently bad-tempered; Ruth apparently suffocating under the weight of a north-eastern accent that, instead of accommodating to her new surroundings, gets thicker by the day; a road about to split the farm; Jill sounding madder each week; Kenton marrying badly; what's-his-name in the College; and now Elizabeth going completely against her past character and having a romp with her previously happily married manager in a tent.

The Archers has had it. There is a whiff of *EastEnders* about what used to be such an enjoyable, simple evening pleasure.

I cannot be the only person who has sadly, but to be honest, with relief, given up the habit.

Lieutenant Commander Nicholas Bradshaw (retd)
Kingsbridge, Devon

SIR — The latest ridiculous storyline in *The Archers* is the final straw: after 45 years of faithful (my children would say fanatical) listening, I have stopped. But what do I do with the spare 15 minutes every evening?

Mary Ann Cameron
Chester

WOMAN'S HOUR

SIR — Before the nation goes into decline over the alleged lack of female broadcasters (I confess, you could have fooled me), should we not be concerned about the all-female team now running BBC Two's *Newsnight* post-Paxman?

Richard Last
Woking, Surrey

SIR – I've never bought into this Jeremy adoration thing. Whether it be Clarkson or Paxman, they have both spent their lives sitting in judgment on their fellow human beings, pointing out how utterly useless they all are compared to them.

Meanwhile, today's movers and shakers remain as devoid of ethics, morality and honesty as they did when Paxman conducted his first interview.

Huw Beynon
Llandeilo, Carmarthenshire

SIR – If Mr Paxman is at a loose end, is there any way he could be persuaded to become Speaker of the House of Commons? It might add a little intellectual rigour and discipline to the proceedings. He might even get a few straight answers.

Robert Langford
Keresley, West Midlands

A YEAR IN
POLITICS

WHIGS, WIZARDS AND WANDERING HANDS

SIR – In view of the current controversy involving Lord Rennard, can we expect a petition retrospectively to withdraw party membership from Messrs Gladstone, Asquith and Lloyd George?

Alistair Dow
Birmingham

SIR – A headline states: 'Lord Rennard could sue his way back into Lib Dem Party.' Pray, why would he bother?

Colin Cummings
Yelvertoft, Northamptonshire

SIR – It comes as a surprise to learn that the Liberal Democrats support *droit du seigneur*.

C.H.
Edinburgh

SIR – I am enjoying every moment of the Rennard saga. It bears out the truth of the old saying: 'He who lives by the Political Correctness dies by the Political Correctness.'

W.G. Sellwood
Stafford

SIR — I do not understand why intelligent, sophisticated women, strong enough to hold down demanding jobs, cannot deal with the wandering hands of a fat, unappealing, personal-space invader without involving everybody else. Sharp, short verbal shrift and a smart swat kept predators at bay in my youth. No real harm done.

At 81 (just) I see the whole Lord Rennard situation as unnecessary and boring old hat. I think the women in question should stop being precious and get on with their jobs.

Dinah Parry
Ottery St Mary, Devon

SIR — Will the police wait until Lord Rennard is 83 before prosecuting him for his alleged sexual misdemeanours?

John D. Ireland
Snainton, North Yorkshire

SIR — I have the greatest sympathy for those charming Lib Dem candidates allegedly harassed by Lord Rennard. Switch to the Conservatives, ladies, and enjoy a hassle-free life.

Jasper Archer
Stapleford, Wiltshire

MORONIC, HOPELESS COALITION

SIR – Lovely oxymoron in your leader today: coalition harmony.

> **Dr John Gladstone**
> Gerrards Cross, Buckinghamshire

SIR – The Prime Minister thinks benefit cuts give people hope. As the Government politicians have suffered no benefit cuts, is that why they are so hopeless?

> **P.H.**
> Bristol

SIR – In 2013 I wrote the following letter which made it into *Am I Missing Something . . . ?*:

'What with the upturn in the economy, Abu Qatada, Andy Murray, The Ashes and Labour's squabbles, I bet David Cameron is regretting creating fixed-term Parliaments.'

Those were all positives at the time.

I make no apologies for resending it to you but now with the addition of current negatives: gay marriage, bedroom tax, wishy-washy sound-bites, Patrick Mercer, Labour's re-emergence, the Lib Dem's refusal of boundary changes, UKIP, the

European elections and, of course, the Scottish referendum.

The bet is still on.

John Tilsiter
Radlett, Hertfordshire

FISHY FIGURES

SIR – Alex Salmond announced on Wednesday that 'every man, woman and child would be £1,000 a year better off if Scotland became independent. That's £2,000 for every family.' Could he please give us a definition of a Scottish family and an explanation of the new maths he is employing?

James Barry
Stokesley, North Yorkshire

SIR – Are there any figures available which reveal how many people switch off their television as soon as Alex Salmond appears?

Stuart Roberts
Southport, Merseyside

SIR – Alex Salmond knows he's got David Cameron by the balls. A little reciprocal castration will not go amiss. I think the Scots would better appreciate a man who stands up and fights.

Joseph G. Dawson
Withnell, Chorley

SIR – Do Mr Salmond and the SNP anticipate that Scotland would walk away from the UK, truly independent and self-supporting, or would they be more like some teenagers, without a job, living on Dad and Mum at home for an indefinite period?

A. John Corbett
Newbury, Berkshire

SIR – As an Englishman, I think it would be a backward step for Scotland to leave the Union, but if the Scots do decide to break away, please can we keep Carol Kirkwood?

Gordon Carter
Halesowen, West Midlands

SIR – I watched the 1966 World Cup Final in Glasgow as the only Englishman in the room.
   Until that time I had no idea how much the Scots hated the English.

John Martin
Ipswich, Suffolk

SIR – May I suggest that the Government takes a leaf out of Putin's book and sends troops to Scottish cities to mingle with the citizens. This would reassure them that they are being protected from the possibility of becoming an independent state.

W.K. Wood
Bolton, Lancashire

SIR – If, as suggested, Kiev were compensated by Russia for the loss of Crimea after it voted to leave Ukraine, how much compensation ought London to be paid by the EU if it annexed Scotland after a vote to leave the UK?

Richard Shaw
Dunstable, Bedfordshire

JUNCKER'S HEROICS

SIR – It's a little disappointing if the worst the sceptics can find to say about Jean-Claude Juncker, the potential President of the European Commission, is that he has cognac for breakfast. If true, it is a foible which would have endeared him to Dr Johnson, who wrote: 'Claret is the liquor for boys, port for men, but he who aspires to be a hero must drink brandy.'

Charles Keen
Duntisbourne Rouse, Gloucestershire

SIR – The good news about the appointment of Juncker is that he seems well qualified to organise a booze-up in a brewery – one task, among many, that has eluded the Commission since its inception.

Richard Endacott
Reading, Berkshire

SIR – Is any information available on the travel plans of Crown Prince Jean-Claude Juncker this coming Saturday, 28 June 2014?

Paul Gregory
Berlin, Germany

SIR – Walking up the High Street in Newport, Shropshire, one Saturday morning in 1941 with friends from a nearby school, we saw a lorry loaded with the remains of a German Junker 88 bomber. We could not resist helping ourselves to a small souvenir.

Should I offer the broken fragment of a Junker's

fuselage to the Prime Minister to brighten the Cabinet Room table?

Sydney Preston
Sevenoaks, Kent

SIR – Although I hate to admit it, I have to side with EU chief Jean-Claude Juncker when he says David Cameron has no common sense. Cameron may have had an Eton education, but he has zilch up top. No way would I trust him on the battlefield. He would be a disaster.

Lt Col Dale Hemming-Tayler (retd)
Edith Weston, Rutland

VINTAGE CLEGG

SIR – Norman Clegg, *Last of the Summer Wine*. Nick Clegg, last of the Lib Dems?

John Ley-Morgan
Weston-super-Mare, Somerset

SIR – Miriam Clegg would be much better suited to holding the office of Deputy Prime Minister than her anarchic husband, who like Ed Miliband, does not believe in either God or the British constitution or anything of permanent value.

Mrs Clegg is highly intelligent, a Christian, and lights up this country with her radiant Spanish smile as she goes about her business. She clearly does not stand any nonsense from her husband, so why should the rest of us?

Timothy Stroud
Salisbury, Wiltshire

SIR – I do feel there is a Liberal part in all of us and have found that life is far better if that part is addressed, first thing in the morning, on a daily basis.

Joss Burn
Tichborne Down, Hampshire

SIR – The Clegg–Farage debate missed one fundamental difference between the UK and Europe. In Europe, if it's not written down, you can't do it. In Britain, if it's not written down, you can do it. We'll never get on with them.

Robert Pleming
Alresford, Hampshire

SIR – Interesting that Nick Clegg always refers to 'Nigel Farage' while Nigel Farage always refers to 'Nick'. Who is correct?

> **G.S.**
> London SE22

THIS VOTER'S NOT FOR TURNING

SIR – To those who are taken in by Mr Farage I would say: you kip if you wish but I am staying awake.

> **Uta Thompson**
> Kew, Surrey

SIR – When I am an old woman, I shall not wear purple – in case people fear I'm a UKIP supporter.

> **Carol Molloy**
> Bovey Tracey, Devon

SIR – Did you read about that French performance artist whose act included a dance at a festival with a live rooster attached to his penis? On being convicted of indecent exhibitionism he claimed that the French do not understand art.

It seems to me that they share our views and it will not therefore be necessary to vote for UKIP.

Clive Pilley
Westcliff-on-Sea, Essex

SIR – Is there a chance that if Nigel Farage gets in, we might be able to smoke in pubs and drink affordable beer again?

Martin Thurston
Liphook, Hampshire

SIR – If UKIP's policies were to be carried out on immigration how would the nation's cars be washed?

Bill Jolly
Lancaster

SIR – UKIP councillor David Silvester's comment that the recent floods are God's wrath at gay marriage legislation brings to mind the serious remark I heard in mid-Wales in the 1970s after we experienced a vigorous earth tremor: 'It's all because of this Sunday football.'

Geoff Neale
Cheltenham, Gloucestershire

SIR — If there is truth behind Councillor Silvester's claims, I would shudder to think what Noah was running away from.

Iain McKie
Totland Bay, Isle of Wight

THE WRONG SORT OF WATER

SIR — When I heard this morning on the news that they were suspending the rail service in the West Country I did not anticipate they meant literally.

Mark Wade
Woodley, Berkshire

SIR — Is there any truth in the rumour of an alleged sighting of Somali pirates at large on the Somerset levels?

David McCreadie
Liphook, Hampshire

SIR — Looks like the Somerset Levels may one day become known as the Somerset Stilts.

Joseph G. Dawson
Withnell, Lancashire

SIR – Would it be sacrilegious to wonder if there was a connection between the Church Commissioners' decision to 're-house' the Bishop of Bath and Wells and the current apocalyptic floods in that area?

> **J.C. Craig**
> Bodmin, Cornwall

SIR – In the good old days we blamed God for catastrophes like this. Now we are secular and there is no God, so we blame the politicians.
    And they don't like it.

> **Roger Antolik**
> Warminster, Wiltshire

SIR – 'At a meeting of Cobra . . .'? Good God, where do they think they are? A Bond movie? If it was 'At a meeting of "Pull our finger out" or "Get off our arse now" . . .' that would have a lot more gravitas.

> **Joseph G. Dawson**
> Withnell, Lancashire

SIR – How many meetings of Cobra have taken place with regard to the flooding in Somerset? It is now seen to be a complete misnomer. Should it be renamed 'Slow Worm'?

> **Mark Harland**
> Scarborough, North Yorkshire

SIR – A Danish zoo was going to send us a giraffe, soon the only creature able to keep its head above water in this sodden isle – and then they shot it. Is Lord Smith one of the zoo's governors?

Michael Begg
Strathconon, Ross-shire

SIR – May I suggest that when the government of Bongo Bongo land sends us relief aid for the floods in Somerset, we should use the money to get a presidential jet for David Cameron.

Julian Shaw
Braintree, Essex

SIR – I see that in today's paper David Cameron and Nigel Farage wear green Wellington boots, while Ed Miliband and Boris Johnson wear black ones. Does this tell us something?

Veronica Bliss
Compton, Hampshire

SIR – Channel 4 anchor-man Jon Snow was interviewing flood victims in Berkshire yesterday. Standing waist deep in water with a clearly distressed couple outside their ruined house, he remarked: 'This is nothing compared to what happens in Bangladesh. When the rains come there . . .

whoosh! . . . everything just gets completely washed away.'

The couple looked at him as though he was mad, which of course he is.

Clearly he still can't get his leftie mind away from disasters in foreign countries, which he obviously considers more worthy of attention than the tragedy taking place in his own country.

The man should be crated and exported.

Malcolm Parkin
Kinnesswood, Kinross

SIR – I note the name of ITV's chief reporter on the Somerset floods: Dan Rivers.

Anthony Rodriguez
Staines Upon Thames, Middlesex

SIR – It strikes me that our weather has not been the same since the Large Hadron Collider. I would therefore suggest that, if it is still on, it be switched off, and if it is not on, it be powered up again and its previous works reversed. Perhaps the jet stream will then settle back where it is meant to be.

Anthony Lee
Wells, Somerset

SIR — I blame Pietersen for the floods.

Bernard Lane
Barford St Michael, Oxfordshire

PATCHY ECONOMIC GROWTH

SIR — Peter Jones has sold out of elbow patches.
This says a great deal about the economic state of
Britain.

Annabel Vetch
London SW6

SIR — As a result of the Chancellor's budget,
I watched my shares in Aviva and William Hill
plummet yesterday (thanks a bunch, George). My
only consolation was that Ed Miliband's credibility
plummeted even further.

Tony Bullock
Kirby Le Soken, Essex

SIR — Am I alone in noticing the ever-increasing
patch of grey hair on Ed's head? It looks unnatural
and he should dye it. Or does he?

Anthony Barnes
Keston, Kent

SIR — Blow my pension fund on a Lamborghini? I think not. Like most over-55s, even if I could get into one, I certainly wouldn't be able to get out.

Michael Gilbert
Beaconsfield, Buckinghamshire

SIR — It is surprising that a cabinet minister is of the opinion that a foreign-built 'supercar' is the aspiration of those due to retire. Surely support for similar British built cars, such as Bentley, McLaren and Noble, would be more appropriate?

Charles Miller
Whitchurch, Shropshire

SIR — Before Lamborghini add an additional night shift, they should wait until George Osborne's next budget tells us pensioners when we will be rich enough to insure one.

Brian Christley
Abergele, Conwy

WE'VE NEVER HAD IT SO GOOD

SIR — We are told that we are living in a state of depressed disposable income, compounded by wage rises being less than inflation.

How is it then that 175,000 persons, predominantly in their teens and twenties, have sufficient uncommitted income as to be able to spend £215 to buy a Glastonbury entrance ticket, plus around twice this on travel and living expenses whilst there?

Harold Macmillan once said: 'You have never had it so good.' This might well be a fair reflection on the present day.

John Jukes
Bosherston, Pembrokeshire

SIR – In the late 1990s our younger daughter, studying GCSE Sociology, came across a definition of poverty as 'not having Sky TV'. We are delighted that we still live in poverty.

Charles and Lesley Greenhough
Rickinghall, Suffolk

SIR – Is a foreign holiday compulsory these days?

Michael Watts
Penrith, Cumbria

SIR – There are some occasions when my husband can become overly excited, and this morning was one of them; he has been notified by the Pensions Service that he will be receiving an additional 25 pence, per week, on reaching his 80th birthday later this year.

He is now eagerly awaiting the chance to have a free cup of latte every eight weeks or so, or even better, put it towards a 2nd class stamp.

Life at 80 can't get much better.

Judy Davey
Harpenden, Hertfordshire

RIP, TONY BENN

SIR – I am sure Tony Benn would have approved – albeit with some hesitation, a wry smile and a puff on his pipe – of the posthumous honour of resting overnight in the Chapel of St Mary Undercroft in the Palace of Westminster.

I suspect, however, he would not like to be on precisely the same resting place as Mrs Thatcher and wonder, when arrangements are made, if he could be positioned somewhat – possibly considerably – to her left.

John Pankhurst
West Bridgford, Nottinghamshire

SIR – If there's a ten-day backlog at the Pearly Gates, what must the waiting room be like with

both Bob Crow and Tony Benn already there,
and now with Clarissa Dickson Wright joining
them?

I'd pay good money to watch that scrap.

Graham Hoyle
Baildon, West Yorkshire

SIR – That Tony Benn escaped denigration for his
social origin while old Etonians in Government do
not is all in accordance with time-honoured British
tradition. Right-wingers born to privilege are
called toffs; left-wingers born to privilege are called
intellectuals, despite the frequent absence of either
breeding or intelligence respectively.

A plague on both their houses. If only it were
a question merely of what you knew or where
you were born that mattered in British politics;
instead it is who you know and what you can do for
them.

The incestuous world of the Westminster
establishment resembles more a Tudor court than a
modern meritocracy.

Jim Doar
Winterborne Houghton, Dorset

SORRY SEEMS TO BE THE SHORTEST WORD

SIR – I have heard a whisper that a rarely performed Noel Coward play, 'Mrs Miller's Apology', is to be revived in the West End with Dame Maggie Smith and Benedict Cumberbatch in the leading roles. Can this really be true? I am told that the play is so short there isn't time for an interval drink.

G.S. Lamb
Croydon, Surrey

SIR – If Cameron's survival is linked to the retention of those boasting the modest talents of Maria Miller, God help him. If she is considered to be a vital member of Government, God help us all.

Robin Potter
Lambston, Pembrokeshire

SIR – The obvious way for the Prime Minister to refute the charge of hypocrisy with regards to Maria Miller is to introduce a Bill redefining the word *hypocrisy* – just as he has redefined the word *marriage*.

Fr Francis Coveney
London E18

SIR — As the Maria Miller case and her astonishingly lenient treatment by a Commons committee proves, there is nothing new under the sun.

Sellar and Yeatman, in their definitive work on English history, *1066 and All That*, wrote that the principal clause of Magna Carta was that barons should be tried only by a jury of other barons, who would understand.

It seems that English governance has advanced little in 799 years.

Peter Croft
Cambridge

SIR — Having read the coverage of Mrs Miller's expenses, I wonder how many people share a similar, wistful wish: I sit and wonder whether the pharmaceutical industry could not come up with a sweet-tasting ambrosia, irresistible to all those in government or with public responsibilities (similar to the effect that opportunities to acquire taxpayers' money seems to have on them), which, like a selective weed killer, would remove from among us all those with self-serving or corrupt motives.

Though perhaps grieved for by their nearest and dearest, at least the long-suffering majority would be spared their poisonous machinations.

We might at last have representatives worthy of our trust.

Ah me! Dreams, dreams.

Robert Sare
Chigwell, Essex

A WORTHY ADDITION TO THE HOUSE

SIR – Oh please, Boris, do become an MP. We need you to make up our full set of prats.

Bill Thompson
Wirral

SIR – With regards to copycat North Korean hairstyles, thank goodness Boris Johnson isn't the crazed dictator of Britain.

Wendy Lay
Brockenhurst, Hampshire

SIR – I would like Lords reform on two conditions.
One, none of them is under the age of 35.
Two, none of them has ever sat in the House of Commons.

J.D.
Taunton, Devon

SIR — Having just opened the paper to be confronted by a photo of MPs preparing for the London Marathon, I would like to thank the men who have the good taste to run in loose, long shorts.

Felicity Foulis Brown
Bramley, Hampshire

SIR — I find myself uncharacteristically aligned with the opinion of Sally Bercow; she has declared she no longer wants to be in the spotlight.

Peter Wickison
Bluntisham, Cambridgeshire

SIR — Following the difficulties that Nigella Lawson has had with entering the US, I would like to draw readers' (and US immigration authorities') attention to the splendidly comprehensive list of MPs who have admitted to inhaling the odd spliff. A quick shufti on Google will reveal all.

David Ellis
Tarves, Aberdeenshire

TROJAN HORSE TIP OFF

SIR – Your article on the so-called Trojan Horse plot in Birmingham schools reminds me that in the 1960s I was seconded to work in Tanzania a couple of years after their independence. I came into contact with the indigenous population, Hindus, Sikhs and Muslims, with whom I enjoyed working.

Large numbers of the Muslims said that they would try and get to England, for they had been ruled for 100 years by the British and in 100 years they would rule Britain.

This disturbed me so much that I wrote twice to the then Prime Minister, Harold Wilson. I did not receive a reply to either of my letters.

The Trojan Horse incident does not surprise me.

Tom Wainwright
Aughton, Lancashire

SIR – I note the suggestion that 'super-heads' are the answer to the woes of these troubled schools. Would that be *super* as in superfluous or supernumerary or possibly supercilious?

Mike Morris
Old Swinford, West Midlands

SIR – Let me see now. Unmoving and rigid? Tick. Wooden head? Tick. Hidden agenda? Tick. Oh dear, the Trojan Horse is actually Michael Gove.

John Tavner
Dedham, Essex

GOVE'S STICKY WICKET

SIR – Is Michael Gove the Kevin Pietersen of the Conservative party?

Barrie Middleton
Matlock, Derbyshire

SIR – Addressing the books which students may read, Michael Gove says, 'If they wish to include Steinbeck . . . no one would be more delighted than me.'

This from a graduate in English literature!

Alan M. Pardoe
Malvern Wells, Worcestershire

SIR – Mr Gove believes that every child should be the 'author of their own life story', whatever that may mean. In any case, a child is singular and thus can write only his or her life story.

'Why can't the English teach their children how to speak?' Over to you, Mr Education Secretary.

Derek Golding
Frome, Somerset

SIR – After reading about Michael Gove's latest idea of training teachers to teach Latin and Greek in every school, I thought this really demands a letter. Unfortunately, words fail me.

David Brown
Preston, Lancashire

SIR – I am delighted that Michael Gove intends to make state schools as good as private but I wish he would hurry up. I am paying for my four children to go to independent schools and it's not cheap.

Mark Solon
London N1

SIR – With regards to taking children out of school during term time there is a very simple solution: let the parents take their holiday and allow our esteemed Education Secretary to look after the children himself. That way he can demonstrate his unquestionable skills.

Vincent Mann
Thornbury, Gloucestershire

SIR — The photograph of Michael Gove at a school in Edmonton was interesting from a teacher's point of view. If you study the photograph closely, you notice that only three of the children in the group appear to be taking any notice of what he is saying. Even the other adult present is looking away.

An Ofsted inspector would not be impressed by his ability to command attention in the classroom. It's not as easy as you think.

Dr Richard Greenfield
Mildenhall, Suffolk

SIR — If David Cameron had a wicked sense of humour he'd sack Michael Gove and replace him with an Old Etonian.

Charles Shea-Simonds
Upavon, Wiltshire

SIR — My grandson is under the impression that, in his new job, Michael Gove will be patrolling the Houses of Parliament with a whip in his hands.

Eddie Peart
Rotherham, South Yorkshire

SIR – The BBC announced that Michael Gove has been replaced by Nicky Morgan, a 'working mother'. However, there was no mention that Ms Morgan was replacing Mr Gove, a 'working father'.

Clara Magill
Lisburn, Co Antrim, Northern Ireland

CABINET GIRLS

SIR – Much to my surprise, I have not yet received details of my new Cabinet post. I cannot understand this as I know I meet the exacting criteria for high office: I am a woman.

Judith A. Scott
St Ives, Cambridgeshire

SIR – Can we now expect the Cabinet Office to publish a Calendar Girls style calendar for next year? Surely that will encourage those wavering voters?

Jenny Severn
Darlington, Co Durham

SIR – How typical that the self-publicising Esther McVey should pose for the Downing Street cameras. And how typical that the *Telegraph* should show her, full length, in the front-page glamour slot.

Bill Davidson
Balderton, Nottinghamshire

SIR – If the public's perception of politicians is one of self-serving greed and incompetence, at least the latest reshuffle has one positive outcome. As a middle-aged, heterosexual male the new Cabinet is more pleasing to the eye.

Neil Webster
Fulwood, Lancashire

SIR – David Cameron wants fewer middle-aged, white men in the Cabinet; what a pity he didn't lead by example and step down himself.

David Lane
Birmingham

SIR – The night of the blunt knives?

Peter Mugridge
Epsom, Surrey

SIR – As part of this ministerial reshuffle, and amid the continuing fallout from Butler-Sloss, Trojan Horses and radical prison imams, should not Mr Cameron have considered appointing a Minister for Unintended Consequences?

Adrian Rowbotham
Eridge Green, East Sussex

UNINTENDED CONSEQUENCES OF GAY MARRIAGE

SIR – My lifelong pal and I are both divorced, with grandchildren, and in our late sixties. We now share a flat and although not homosexual, have been advised that there would be tax benefits if we got married. Could you kindly inform me if we would have to declare ourselves as homosexual in order to qualify?

E.J.
Bath

SIR – Philip Hammond, the Defence Secretary, has said that Tories against gay marriage must move on. I have moved on; I no longer vote Tory.

Anne Ellis
Bishops Sutton, Hampshire

SIR – Look on the bright side: heterosexual couples can celebrate a broader repertoire for the consummation of their union thanks to the legislation of gay marriage.

D.P.
London E2

SIR – No matter what your viewpoint on gay weddings, does this mean that the phrase, 'He never married' at the end of obituaries is now redundant? It was a very English way of being respectful and informative without being judgmental.

Philip Moger
East Preston, West Sussex

THE USE AND
ABUSE OF
LANGUAGE

HAVE A GOOD DAY

SIR – Having just read the letters about waiters saying 'Enjoy', I thought I must tell you that I went into our local cut-price chemists to buy some loo rolls and the young man, as he handed them to me, said, 'Enjoy.'

I replied: 'I'll try.'

Graham Upton
Eastbourne, East Sussex

SIR – A number of years ago, in a store in California, a dear friend, on taking his receipt from the young, pretty but obviously disaffected sales girl, asked her, 'Aren't you going to say, "Have a nice day"?'

Her reply: 'It says it on the f****** ticket.'

Peter Nicholson
Glasgow

SIR – For nearly five years I endured my office manager's nightly, 'See you later', when I had little desire to socialise with him out of hours.

However, when leaving the office for the final time after being made redundant, my response to his final cheery farewell is probably not suitable for a family newspaper.

E.C.
Brighton, West Sussex

RHYMING CLARKLETS

SIR — I fail to see what the fuss is about Jeremy Clarkson. As I recall, the rhyme went: *Eeny meeny, miny mo, sit the baby on the po, when he's done, wipe his bum, show his mother what he's done.*

What's offensive about that?

Josie Jeffrey
Little Gaddesden, Herefordshire

SIR — Jeremy Clarkson should have used the word *whatsit*. 'Catch a whatsit by the toe' has a certain Edward Lear-esque magic to it that stimulates and intrigues the imagination.

Whatsit is also politically correct — at least for now.

B.D.
Swansea

SIR — I would like to jump on the Jeremy Clarkson bandwagon and suggest that the voters who call me a Nazi when I am canvassing for the Conservative party are held to account.

J. Perkins
Whitstable, Kent

SIR — Given the alacrity with which the BBC sanctioned both Carol Thatcher and Jeremy

Clarkson I find it a shame that they could not act with such speed over the very serious transgressions of Jimmy Savile.

Stephen Barklem
Woking, Surrey

BYE FOR NOW, BBC

SIR – There was a time when the English spoken by those on BBC was considered perfect. Now we have news readers saying 'okay', meaning 'alright', 'see you later' and 'bye for now'. English has always been a growing language, but there should be limits.

B.A. Henderson
Woodcote, Berkshire

SIR – We've recently been told by several weather forecasters that the ground is 'very saturated'. Is that not like describing someone as 'very pregnant'?

Andrew Blake
Shalbourne, Wiltshire

SIR – I wonder if anyone else found it immensely irritating to listen to the BBC commentators' ill-command of the English language during the Sochi Games (Clare Balding excluded). One is never 'sat' in third place, nor is one 'stood' in the nearest gate.

Please give them a basic lesson in good grammar to save the bleeding ears of the British public.

I am not an old biddy complaining; I am a 28-year-old shop girl.

Annabella Forbes
London SW7

SIR – Before the endin' of the Winter Olympics, can BBC commentators be told not to pronounce any 'g' in words ending 'ing'? Am I the only one that finds it just a little bit annoyin'?

James Thacker
Tanworth in Arden, Warwickshire

SIR – ITV commentator at the World Cup: 'Iranians often display their Christian name on their shirts.'

Really? I think not.

Tony Elliott
Wargrave, Berkshire

SIR – Was I alone in hearing a BBC reporter saying, 'Covers at Centre Court Wimbledon are being deflated down'? What?

Jonathan F. Nason
Kings Bromley, Staffordshire

SIR – Listening to the commentary it appears that the Duchess of Cambridge 'loves her tennis'. Why only her tennis?

Wendy Richards
Enstone, Oxfordshire

SIR – It is interesting that Mark Petchey is referred to as Petch by the other Wimbledon commentators. Had his name been Petch, he would probably have been called Petchey.

Peter Hamilton
London SE3

SIR – Is there no end to the Americanisation of our once proud English tongue? At Wimbledon they are now taking 'a bathroom break'. I would have thought four minutes to get undressed, take a bath and get dressed again was beyond belief.

R.M. Flaherty
Auchterarder, Kinross

SIR – On Friday I was quietly reading *The Daily Telegraph* while my daughter was watching the tennis. Suddenly she said, 'Wow, wonderful Justin.'

I asked who was Justin.

She said, 'Dad, it was a wonderful shot; the ball was just in.'

Is this normal?

Nick Hawksley
Ashill, Somerset

SIR — I think it is about time that someone complained about the affectation of television presenters pushing their tongues forward when they speak. In some cases it is so bad that sibilance is impossible.

Could I recommend that public speakers carry out speaking exercises involving the words *Shibboleth* (which I understand was a test word in the distant past) and *Blitz*. When they feel they can say these words clearly without spraying everything in the vicinity with saliva they should consider themselves cured.

Thank you in anticipation of your printing of this important message.

J. Taylor
Rotherham, South Yorkshire

SIR – Your correspondent asks how to pronounce 'Ms'. This is very easy to answer. Ms is, of course, an onomatopoeic modern term used both as an unmarried lady's title and the sound of a wasp trapped in a jam jar.

Andrew H.N. Gray
Edinburgh

HOW TO ADDRESS A FEMALE CHAIR

SIR – How much more credence your correspondent gives her letter by styling herself as 'Chairman', rather than the wishy-washy, PC title 'Chair'. Someone who presides at a meeting is Chairman, regardless of their gender, in the same way that dog owners are dog owners, even if their animal happens to be a bitch.

When I see letters from people who sign themselves as 'Chair' I think: I wish I hadn't bothered to read that.

Robin Graham
Broughton, Cambridgeshire

SIR – Why don't we simply address each other as 'my old fruit'? That is not sexist.

Alan Sabatini
Bournemouth, Dorset

SIR – I suggest the miserable souls who moan about being called 'love' and 'darling' stay at home in their windy garrets and stick pins in themselves.

Much love,

Alison Williams
Ipswich, Suffolk

IMPOVERISHED ENGLISH

SIR – Either the perceived pressure of life or a lack of manners result in phrases such as 'grab a sandwich', 'grab a train' (how, exactly?) and 'grab a few minutes' sleep' (does one ask: from whom?).

In an attempt at friendly informality we also hear, 'just pop your PIN in' (usually followed by 'for me'), 'pop out for a drink', 'pop the cake in the oven' – and a myriad others.

How sad that the English language should be so impoverished.

Anne Osborne
Ringwood, Hampshire

SIR – While we are on the subject of irritating words and phrases, is anyone else irked by being offered a 'regular' coffee when medium is meant? I have a regular coffee, daily, in the afternoon.

Peter Wickison
Bluntisham, Cambridgeshire

A CUT-HEDGE ACCENT

SIR – I was woken this morning by two gardeners next door whose accents were so affectedly common, and their banter so volubly banal (think Harry and Paul parody *EastEnders*), that it was a relief when they turned on the high-powered, petrol-driven 210dB hedge cutter.

Why make such an effort to speak so badly? I do at least understand Jacob Rees-Mogg.

Sam Glen
Colchester, Essex

AUTHORITATIVE MPS AND OTHER OXYMORONS

SIR – George Osborne really needs to learn how to say *authoritative*. Twice in his interview on Radio 4 this morning he pronounced it as 'authoritive' – there is no such word.

Rob Turnbull
Hutton Rudby, North Yorkshire

SIR – I have always found the term 'industrial action' to be something of an oxymoron. Those on strike on Thursday weren't from industry, nor were they being active.

Anthony Pickles
Penarth, Glamorgan

SIR – How is one expected to give credence to politicians, this one educated at Westminster no less, who come out with sentences such as Nick Clegg's: 'I think the answer that UKIP and other people who want to withdraw ourselves from what is the world's largest economy . . .'
I had to switch off.

C.A. Delahunty
London W2

SIR – Am I alone in being intensely irritated by Nick Clegg's habit of pronouncing the word *create* as 'crate', which is now being copied by many people in the media?

Alan Blaiden
London SW20

SIR – Is anyone else heartily sick of the New Labour glottal stop or is it just me?

Stephen Howard
Aldershot, Surrey

SIR – Here's a little thought for the new session of Parliament: every time MPs start a sentence with 'Look . . .,' they should donate a pound to a hardship fund for pensioners. I am confident that our senior citizens will be feasting on caviar and champagne by the end of the year.

Graham McCann
Cambridge

EXONERATED UNTIL PROVEN GUILTY

SIR – I am puzzled that recent reporting of a high-profile court case says that a defendant has been 'cleared' and 'exonerated'. I was not aware that such verdicts were possible. Not guilty is not necessarily the same as innocent.

Gregor Macaulay
Dunedin, New Zealand

SIR – Can you or one of your readers please explain to me the difference between 'denying' and 'strongly denying' an allegation?

Richard Veal
Binfield, Berkshire

SUB EDITORS AND WIVES BOUGHT TO BOOK

SIR – I often chastise my wife for mistakenly using the word *bought* instead of *brought*. I find this to be a common mistake among the English population at large. Can you imagine my astonishment when I discovered that even *The Daily Telegraph* doesn't know the difference?

Cassius C. Chanides
Brackley, Northamptonshire

SIR – You report that: 'Every school will be ordered to actively promote British values.' Will that include not splitting the infinitive?

Paul Eward
Ross-on-Wye, Herefordshire

SIR – Have I Alzheimer's? The constant repetition in reports makes one wonder if the paper is geared to those who need to be told something twice over.

Mrs D. Tallack
Ringwood, Hampshire

SIR – In answering 'No' to 'Should children be banned from museums?', your columnist refers to 'Britain, with it's [sic] most wonderful, rich, vibrant museums and galleries'. It is hard to believe that 66 per cent of your readers would agree with someone who misuses an apostrophe.

David Townson
Isleworth, Middlesex

SIR – You published an article describing a small storm-in-a-tea-cup caused by a forthcoming film about Noah which omitted any reference to God. I found it ironic that you wrote about the 'huge replica arc' being built. Would it be unfair to suggest that ignorance of matters Biblical is not confined to film-makers?

Dr Martin Shutkever
Pontefract, West Yorkshire

SIR – I applaud Allison Pearson's article in which she champions the case for the correct use of the English language. She admits, however, that when writing her column she may slip in a deliberate mistake or two to defy Cruel Fate and give multiple orgasms to all her loyal nitpickers.

As one of her loyal nitpickers, male, aged 72, and not prone to multiple orgasms, I can only assume that she deliberately slipped in such a mistake today in an attempt to turn me on. I refer to her use of the word *kid*.

To paraphrase her final sentence, when I see the word *kid*, which used to mean baby goat instead of child, something inside me dies.

Peterjon Dodd
Womersley, North Yorkshire

TEACHING AND DAYDREAMING

SIR — Allison Pearson's article on educational 'blobbledegook' reminded me of when I worked as a teaching assistant. At the beginning of each term we were assembled to hear the pearls of wisdom distilled from the staff meeting. On one occasion we were told that the focus for the term would be 'teaching and learning'. Really? In a school?

Jennie Gibbs
Goring by Sea, West Sussex

SIR — As a young, newly qualified teacher struggling to write my first set of reports, I was made aware of the succinct writing skills of the very experienced Head of Science. One particularly impressive effort read thus: 'Warms the seat'.

Mary Morley
Ashford, Kent

PITFALLS OF PITMAN

SIR — When I worked as a secretary in a Medical Social Work Department, the social workers used to dictate the notes for us to type up. I well remember the record of a professional legal gentleman whose wife was concerned at an aspect of their private life.

The summary went: 'Main problem appears to be husband on trains nights.'

Anyone who knows the New World version of Pitman's shorthand would recognise some very sloppy shorthand outlines. What it should have been transcribed as was: 'Main problem appears to be husband a transvestite.'

Sue Bowman
Bristol

SIR – It is not only patients who have a poor grasp of medical language. When I trained as a nurse in the 1970s, hospital doctors understood the Latin origins of words used in prescriptions, such as *nocte* for 'at night' and *mane* for 'in the morning'.

Nowadays the letter 'e' in these words is routinely adorned with a French acute accent.

Simon Pike
Hoarwithy, Herefordshire

SIR – On opening an appointment letter from our local hospital I noticed I was to report to the 'Geriatrics' department, which made my blood boil slightly.

A few weeks later, on a return visit to the same department, the name had changed to 'General

Medicine and Care of the Older Person' — a much kinder pseudonym.

The only time *geriatric* is used in our house is when I have beaten my husband at Scrabble three times running, and have achieved my Gerry-hat-trick.

Audrey Bowler
Whiteball, Somerset

SIR — Scrabble is much more competitive in our house. The other day my wife offered certain favours for a letter I held. I declined and won the game.

Michael Hockey
Chiselborough, Somerset

FIX US

SIR — With regards to the 'conscious uncoupling' of Gwyneth and Chris Martin, which poor soul is going to be lumbered with that CD collection?

Marlon Zoglowek
Cam, Gloucestershire

SIR – One can only assume the lovemaking between the famous pair was unconscious coupling.

Bob Ringwood
Winchelsea Beach, East Sussex

HIGHWAY CODES

SIR – I wonder if any of your readers has come across a more apt or amusing business name than the one I saw yesterday on the roof of a driving school car: 'L-Passo.'

Bruce Chalmers
Goring by Sea, West Sussex

SIR – Driving in Somerset we were interested to see a cleaning van with the sign: 'No toilet rolls kept in van overnight.'

David and Pauline Laughton
Chard, Somerset

SIR – Margaret Thatcher's most insidious legacy is a change to our national psyche that even affects our language. In every bus and railway station the Tannoys blare out, 'This is a customer announcement', without a single voice raised in protest. We, the travelling public, are passengers, not customers.

Mark Evans
London NW1

SIR – Today a small notice was posted on our local post box stating that, 'In order to provide our customers with the best possible service, the collections have been rescheduled.'

The last collection will no longer take place at 5.45 pm, but at 4 pm.

In what Orwellian double-speaking nightmare does 'the best possible service' mean the exact opposite?

S.R.
Gosforth, Newcastle upon Tyne

LEBENSRAUM

SIR – Your correspondent blames Hitler for his mother's shipment of bananas looking like shrivelled black fingers when they finally arrived in Britain in 1944. I am reminded of my father who served with distinction in both world wars. He was sitting in his club (Brooks's) in late April 1945 reading the tickertape strips displayed by the front door.

On one he read Hitler being quoted as saying: 'I cannot shift the responsibility.'

Noticing that the typist had omitted the letter 'f' in the middle word, my father wrote alongside: 'Surely this explains a great deal?'

Hugh Williams
Crapstone, Devon

ALIMENTARY BAD JOKES

SIR — Is it true that Benedict Cumberbatch is planning on exploiting his success in *Sherlock* by opening a chain of restaurants called 'Alimentary'?

I. McC.
Burton in Kendal, Cumbria

SIR — On reading that she has an assisted death pact with her husband, Richard, one must assume that Judy Finnigan, unlike her kinsman, Michael, does not believe that she will beginnigan.

F.A.
Haverfordwest, Pembrokeshire

SIR — It is fitting that AstraZeneca is meeting the latest Pfizer offer with stiff opposition.

J.B.
Slapton, Devon

SIR — There was a discussion on the City News this morning as to what price might be set for shares in the flotation of Poundland. I would have thought the answer was obvious.

R.G.-W.
London SE27

SIR — Your headline informs us: 'Half of Sex Offenders Spared Jail'. Am I right in thinking that would be the upper half?

Col J.P.
Corton Denham, Dorset

NAUGHTY BUT NICE MNEMONICS

SIR — Your readers' mnemonics are all pretty proper so far. I know some that would be too earthy for your respectable publication, but have you any room for the mildly naughty but nice category?

For example, Mr Schober's older physics classes

to remember the order of planets: 'Men very easily make jugs serve useful nocturnal purposes.'

Or, on the back of an envelope from a passionate returning warrior to his sweetheart, 'BURMA' or 'NORWICH'?

Barry Birtwistle
Colne, Lancashire

SIR – With regards to mnemonics, I remember as a medical student being taught 'luscious French tarts sit naked in anticipation'.

I can't for the life of me remember what it stood for.

Dr Angela Lishman
South Shields, Co Durham

SIR – Maybe it is a bit late in the day for more mnemonics, but I have been busy of late. Two come to mind from schooldays, one of which is printable, the other probably not.

The Duke of Marlborough's telephone number: BROM 4689. This relates to his great Battles of Blenheim, Ramillies, Oudenarde and Malplaquet in 1704, 1706, 1708 and 1709.

The second is to remember the cranial nerves of a dogfish: 'Oh! Oh! Oh! To tickle and feel a girl's vagina!'

The nerves are Olfactory, Optic, Oculomotor, Trochlear, Trigeminal, Abductor, Facial, Glosso-pharyngeal and Vagus.

Perhaps the fishy one could make the next edition of your unpublished letters.

Angus Jacobsen
Inverbervie, Angus

SIR – How about this one suggested by an Australian in a book I am reading: 'Rip out your guts before I vomit.'

Morgan Jones
London SW6

HEAVE AWAY EASILY, MEMSAAB

SIR – I seldom carry a wrist watch, having a propensity to lose them. If I need to, I ask my lady wife: *Kitna budja hai?* (What time is it?), a phrase I remember from my time as a deck officer in Indian-crewed ships of the Bocklebank Line of Calcutta Steamers many years ago.

A Glasgow firm, Brown, Son and Ferguson, still prints a booklet, *Malim Sahib's Hindustani,* which gives translations of nautical terms.

Phrases such as *Avis asti* (Heave away easily) or *Bando* (Make fast) are not really useful nowadays. However,

Kitna budja hai? still is, and although my dear wife of English parentage has learnt Welsh proficiently, she is limited to just the one Hindustani phrase.

Sid Davies
Bramhall, Cheshire

SIR — Many years ago my husband ordered a dry martini for me at the bar in the interlude of an opera in Dusseldorf. I was delighted when I was given three.

Isobel Whatrup
Wigmore, Kent

SIR — In the 1960s, my father-in-law, a Yorkshire farmer and dairyman, had his milk bottles inscribed: 'This bottle cost 8d, it's brittle as owt, if tha loss it or brek it, I'm workin for nowt.'

Translation available from the address below.

Ken Grimrod-Smythe
Ingbirchworth, South Yorkshire

SIR — I recently noticed my shower gel had 'Lather and Rinse' written in 17 different languages. I'm so relieved I have been using it correctly for the last 40-odd years.

Peta Braddock
Radcliffe on Trent, Nottinghamshire

SIR – At passport control at Chambery Airport in France I was interested to see that the Russian word for immigration is a letter for letter translation from the English. Does Russia not have immigrants?

Ian Warrington
Cheadle Hulme, Cheshire

HOME
THOUGHTS ON
ABROAD

TALK TALK, NOT WAR, WAR

SIR – There is very little Britain can do to halt
Russian aggression against Ukraine, now that we
have virtually no navy and our tiny but brave army is
disturbingly over-stretched turning out the lights in
Afghanistan.

So we have to use the ultimate weapon at
our disposal: give Mr Putin a subscription to
TalkTalk.

A month dealing with the telecom 'provider'
will reduce even this former KGB hard man to a
gibbering wreck. Imagine: every time Mr Putin
wants to converse with President Obama, his
phone will be re-routed to TalkTalk's billing
department. A heavily accented operator in
the Philippines, bleary eyed from too many
months on the nightshift, will mumble over a
poor quality internet link that Moscow 321 is not
recognised by their database. They'll hang up on
him a few times just for good measure. He'll spend
hours calling a premium rate 0870 number to
cancel the subscription, only to be told – when
he eventually gets through – that their systems are
down.

Four weeks of this hell, all the time exposed to
the incoming cacophony of vacuous, insincere
announcements as he listens to the same 15-second
jingle being painfully carved into his psyche without

anaesthetic, will leave Mr Putin unable even to park his bicycle on the lawn of his neighbour's dacha – let alone ready to order his tanks into Ukraine.

Tim Arnold
Slough, Berkshire

SIR – Is the stand-off between Russia and Ukraine a devious Emirates plot to withdraw Roman Abramovich's visa, put Chelsea into administration and subsequently deduct 10 points?

Jan Bishop
Shrewsbury

SIR – The UK should nationalise Chelsea football club in response.

Russell Jackson
Ewloe, Flintshire

SIR – It is reported that McDonald's have pulled out of Crimea. At least there is something positive for the local population as a result of President Putin's action.

John Sorrell
Paris

SIR — One reads history and wonders how great countries and wise minds drift into wars which take millions of lives. Almost all of pages one, two and three of your paper today concern Mick Jagger. Should Russia invade Ukraine there may again be millions of people who can't get no satisfaction. Good to see you have your priorities right.

Sebastian Neville-Clarke
Horsham, West Sussex

THE AMBASSADOR IS NOT SPOILING US

SIR — Reading your article about the state banquet for the President of Ireland, I noticed the inset showing the menu. Is it just me who finds a 'Bombe Glacée' an interesting choice for this particular gathering?

Dan Scott
Skelton on Ure, North Yorkshire

SIR — *The Daily Telegraph*'s letters on obtaining decent tea abroad have diplomatic implications. While not advocating declarations of war, I do feel that Britain should break off diplomatic relations with states which cannot demonstrate correct tea-making skills or facilities. Alternatively, we should offer tea training by the WI as part of Britain's overseas aid.

Terry Critchley
High Legh, Cheshire

AUX ARMES, SUJETS

SIR — King Juan Carlos of Spain was an excellent monarch who presided over the transition from General Franco's regime to modern constitutional government. Let us hope that his son will be as wise and humane as his father.

In the course of time I believe the French will see the error of their ways, and also restore a constitutional monarchy to France.

Timothy Stroud
Salisbury, Wiltshire

BEND ZE KNEES, MATE

SIR — Boris Johnson asserts that the instructors in the *Ecole du Ski Français* are 'French, mes amis. And only French.' One of the instructors in the ESF in Courchevel 1850, who has been there for many years, is Australian, known locally as Ozzy John.

Oh, and he doesn't wear an all in one suit, either.

Caroline Houseman
Goole, East Yorkshire

DOING A FRENCHIE

SIR – As an ageing xenophobe I have in the past – however irrationally – found it difficult to shout aloud support for anything from across the channel, especially from France. However, your report regarding the French Military Chiefs of Staff has cured me, if only temporarily, of my debility.

How pleasing that their most senior commanders have threatened joint resignation if the French government imposes any more cuts. And what a pity we didn't have a similar show of strength from our own top brass when the coalition embarked on its misguided neutering. Perhaps the Chief of the Defence Staff will now do a 'Frenchie'? Although I doubt it.

Ken Orme
Liverpool

SIR — I was very concerned to hear that 250,000 French people have settled in London. Will they steal our women? Will their bicycle-riding onion sellers undercut our honest greengrocers? Will shifty gangs lurk on street corners, twirling their moustaches and sneering *zut alors* at innocent English passers-by? We deserve to be told.

Ben Barber
London SW10

SIR — France is the country that packs cheeses in boxes designed so that no matter how much one consumes, the remainder will not fit back into the box. It is the country where you get shouted at in a foreign language when you park your car in a huge space clearly marked 'Car'. It is the country so poverty stricken that the occupants of campsites obviously cannot afford clothes. I love it.

David Walker
Windsor, Berkshire

A ROCK AND A HARD PLACE

SIR — I can assure your correspondent that Croatia's rocky shoreline does not guarantee an absence of children. I have witnessed the somewhat incongruous, though not entirely disagreeable, sight of small children, clad in full-length, UV-resistant swimsuits playing at the water's edge, watched over by their young mothers sunbathing au naturel on the rocks behind them.

David Forbes
Edith Weston, Rutland

FIRST AMONG SEQUELS

SIR — The answer to François Hollande's affairs of the heart is that he should abandon the title of First Lady and instead institute First Mistress, Second Mistress and so on.

All of his lady friends would then know where they stand — or lie down.

Ron Mason
East Grinstead, West Sussex

SIR — The domestic difficulties of President Hollande remind me of one of my favourite sayings: 'He who marries his mistress creates a vacancy.'

Jim Brown
Mindrum Mill, Northumberland

SIR — I am reminded of the variant of the old nursery rhyme:

As I was going to St Ives
I met a man with seven wives.
Of course, the seven wives weren't his,
But here in France, that's how it is.

Gilbert Dunlop
Great Offley, Hertfordshire

SIR — Citoyens! Silence, s'il vous plaît. Le Président baise.

James Hazan
Huddersfield, West Yorkshire

SIR — France has François Hollande, Valerie Trierweiler and Julie Gayet. We have John Major, Norma Major and Edwina Curry.

Vive la France!

John Tucker
Torquay, Devon

SIR — Given that François Hollande has a penchant for travelling around Paris anonymously, would it not be an appropriate gift for London's Mayor to send him a Boris Bike?

Patrick Brennan
Stevington, Bedfordshire

SIR — The sight of President Hollande riding a
scooter to visit his mistress is risible. Surely the
man could have chosen a more appropriate form of
transport, such as a Honda Fireblade, a Triumph
Trophy, a Kawasaki ZZR1400 Performance Special
or a Ducati Superleggera?

Paul Strong
Claxby, Lincolnshire

SIR — Observers have reasoned that the crash helmet
worn by the French President to his alleged trysts
is to protect his anonymity. I should have thought
it far more likely that he wears it as a precautionary
measure for when Valerie gets hold of him.

Mike Owen
Claverdon, Warwickshire

SIR — I am reminded of what Kingsley Amis said
when he separated from his second wife: 'Jane made
a condition: that I should give up drink, and then
she'd consider returning. Her second condition was
that I should saw off my head and serve it up with a
little hollandaise sauce.'

Perhaps Valerie Trierweiler should try this
French recipe?

Bernard Richards
Brasenose College, Oxford

SIR – Has anyone considered that Madame Trierweiler might secretly be glad that François Hollande has a new girlfriend?

Anthony M. Day
Alton, Hampshire

SIR – François Hollande looks too much like Bilko for me to take him seriously.

Beatrice Baxter
Ilford, Essex

SIR – President Hollande must have what my late mother-in-law called 'it'. He makes Alan Clark look like a short runner.

Gray Gilbert
Fovant, Wiltshire

SIR – Why should we be interested in François Hollande's sex life, unless it involves Angela Merkel?

John G. Prescott
Coulsdon, Surrey

SIR – Men and women are conceived in the female womb, upon whose nourishment we wholly depend. Men never entirely lose our need for intimacy with females. The penalties for not engaging intimately are low hormonal states, low mood and bad health.

Males, like infants screaming to suckle, can urgently display a desperate need for sexual union.

On the other hand, females, the origin of hormonal reserve, may be content to go longer intervals without sexual intimacy.

I trust this may be of some assistance to your readers perplexed by a French President's activities, and that accordingly, they may refrain from ridiculing him.

P.H.
Newmarket, Suffolk

LIE IN PEACE, SHARON

SIR – Your photograph of Ariel Sharon's coffin carried a caption that included the phrase: 'The former premier, who died 11 January, lied in state at the Knesset, Israel's parliament . . .'

All politicians lie, and some even to parliament, but not after they have died, surely?

Prof Robin Jacoby
Hethe, Oxfordshire

SIR – I noticed that Tony Blair was wearing a kippah at Ariel Sharon's funeral. Did he go the whole way and undergo circumcision before travelling? How much will this hypocrite suffer to be true to his craft?

Lieutenant Colonel Richard King-Evans
Normandy, France

SIR – Are we allowed to know how much Tony Blair charged to give the eulogy at Ariel Sharon's funeral?

Robin Lane
Devizes, Wiltshire

SIR – When reading about the Blairs' property portfolio I couldn't help but think just how profitable socialism can be – provided one is not poor or a member of the general public, of course.

Dr A. Dyson
Southwell, Nottinghamshire

SIR – Tony Blair is alive and Bobby Womack is dead. Now tell me God exists.

T. Maunder
Leeds

SIR — As the situation in the Middle East deteriorates would now be an appropriate time for Tony Blair to reveal his divinity? I am sure that the sight of him descending into Jerusalem in clouds of glory would bring about an instant end to hostilities.

Tony Hines
Longframlington, Northumberland

MADNESS IN THE MIDDLE EAST

SIR — At a time of upheaval in the Middle East it is worth recalling what Lord Salisbury had to contend with as Prime Minister at the end of the 19th century. At home Randolph Churchill, who was suffering from the effects of syphilis, was stirring up political trouble, while in the Sudan the 'mad' Mahdi was leading a revolt against the British Empire.

Lord Salisbury observed: 'Randolph Churchill pretends to be sane but in fact is mad, while the Mahdi pretends to be mad but is actually quite sane.'

It is hard to know who is sane, and who is mad, in the Middle East at the present time.

Timothy Stroud
Salisbury, Wiltshire

SIR –

This so-called 'ISIS' in Iraq.

MUST.

Be ATTACKED

AT ONCE.

With 'Air Attacks'.

MISSILES.

With 'Napalm'.

BURNS.

With 'Polaris'.

A SLOW RADIATION DEATH.

And with biological and chemical weapons.

SUFFERING.

Because they are a threat to THE WHOLE
WORLD.

Essentially, 'ISIS' are 'The British'.

'Tony' Blair's 'New Labour'.

A FASCIST REGIME.

'Nazis'.

Who FAILED.

'Every Dog Needs A Home'.

So too are these b*stards now looking to Iraq, as
'UK 3'.

WHERE THE DEFEATED 'BRITISH' CAN
LIVE LIKE KINGS.

'Nuke' them.

Led as they are by The Special Air Service ('SAS')
Regiment.

These 'Brecon Beacons Donkeys'.

'Andy' McNab.

Known to people in Bristol as 'Jonathan' from 'The Soup Run'.

'Nuke' them.

And rid Planet Earth of this 'Gung Ho'.

'ISIS'?

A bit 'Old Oxford University'.

cc CIA

The Company

'The Key'

US Nuclear Missile 'Silos'

The United Nations

'Interested Parties'

M

HOW TO FIND FLIGHT MH370

SIR – Despite claims that 'dowsing' has no scientific basis, I have myself experienced the extremely powerful force that twisted a forked hazel stick in my hands whenever I crossed a small underground stream when young.

Some dowsers claim an ability to locate hidden objects miles away by dowsing over a large-scale map. That being so, I would suggest that a far cheaper shortcut to finding the missing aircraft might be to ask them to dowse over a chart of the south Indian Ocean.

Richard Shaw
Dunstable, Bedfordshire

SIR – The remoteness of the current search area for MH370 is emphasised by it being the place on world maps that the circular inset map of Antarctica is often put.

Jeremy Holt
Swindon, Wiltshire

SIR – Your report on the co-pilot of the Malaysian flight MH370 detailed the event of two 'blonde' South African tourists joining him in the cockpit on a flight in 2011. As a mundane and literate blonde this concerned me. Are you inferring that indeed blondes have more fun to make the event seem more scandalous? I'm sure brunettes are capable of the same tomfoolery.

Olivia Jones
Wilmslow, Cheshire

SIR – Why is the battery life of the 'pinger' in the 5kg black box only around 30 days, when the battery in my cardiac pacemaker, weighing 40gms, lasts in the region of 10 years?

Dr Steven Langerman
Watford, Hertfordshire

SIR – In the midst of so many conflicting theories in the sad and perplexing story of the missing plane, I am surprised that nobody has proposed that the plane was subjected to alien abduction and is now on some distant planet.

John Breining-Riches
Chagford, Devon

SIR – For more than twelve years, in the aftermath of the terrorist carnage of September 11, 2001, airline passengers have been subjected to intrusive and vastly expensive screenings, searches, delays and aggravation.

None of us knew that in the locked cockpit was a handy and easily accessible lever that would turn off the transponder.

Pamela R. Goldsack
Banstead, Surrey

SIR — A fuel-saving idea: the earth rotates. So why not send passengers or cargo up in an airship, and when the earth has spun round let the airship descend to its intended destination?

Nick Hawksley
Ashill, Somerset

THE ROADS
MUCH
TRAVELLED

PLEASE TAKE ALL YOUR PERSONAL BELONGINGS WITH YOU

SIR – Not having travelled by train for some time, I had not realised that it is now mandatory for every passenger not only to have a ticket, a Big Mac, a Starbucks coffee and a mobile phone (and/or MP3 player), but a cold as well.

The carrying of handkerchiefs, however, seems to be prohibited.

Graham Masterton
Tadworth, Surrey

SIR – Congratulations to Serco on winning the Caledonian Sleeper Service contract. Their experience in tagging could be invaluable in preventing over-night hanky-panky or absconding at Crewe.

John Forrest
Cranleigh, Surrey

SIR – I travelled today by non-stop train from Newcastle to London. I knew when we were passing Durham because of the Cathedral, and York because of the Minster, but I was unable to decipher the blurred names on any of the station signs.

Why aren't place names written in big letters further away from the platforms so that they can be read from moving trains?

James Hughes-Onslow
London SE5

SIR – Should I be able to afford a pensioner's ticket from London to Birmingham when HS2 is complete, I hope the construction team will beat my own visit from the grim reaper.

A diary note has been made for 2026 to let you know the victor.

Douglas Burcham
Leamington Spa, Warwickshire

SIR – Please ignore the naysayers and nimbys. I've done a straw poll and we all think the Government's proposals for an expensive high-speed rail network are fantastic. Carry on!

Emperor Napoleon Bonaparte
Prestwich Mental Hospital, Manchester

DUTCH COURAGE
TO CYCLE IN CAMBRIDGE

SIR – In your article the discovery that cycling to work in Cambridge was 100 times more common than in Merthyr Tydfil was put down to the different attitudes of the local authorities. Could this also be the reason that cycling is more popular in the Netherlands than in the Himalayas?

Dr David Briggs
Corfe Mullen, Dorset

SIR – Yesterday, in Heffer's main bookshop in Cambridge, to obtain a copy of the Official Highway Code involved finding the Theology section.

Alex Hughes
Kenilworth, Warwickshire

SIR – Some countries, particularly in the Far East, seemingly turn a blind eye to motorbikes on the pavements, so perhaps this will be our next step. Why don't we build dedicated lanes for people who walk? We could call them footpaths.

Roger Stokes
Chester

SIR — I don't mind sharing footpaths with cyclists, but I would like it to be mandatory for them to use their bell when they swoop from behind. I would also like a speed restriction on invalid buggies.

Patricia Chalmers
Crawley, West Sussex

SIR — During the Tube strike London's pavements thronged with commuting, exercising people. Whatever next? Spontaneous conversation?

Timothy Davey
Bristol

EXHAUSTING PIPES

SIR — This morning I sat on a bench, smoking a cigarette, next to a main road, reading *The Daily Telegraph* with its coverage of smoking in cars when children are present. Toddlers and children in prams and pushchairs passed with their heads at about the same level as the exhaust pipes of hundreds of cars.

If exhaust fumes were as visible as cigarette smoke there would be a campaign to ban the car. Is there any reason why the exhaust pipes should not come out of the tops of cars?

Barry Gee
Plymouth, Devon

SIR – Smoking in cars? I appear to have survived the Romeo y Julietta cigar and Players non-tipped cigarette smoke in the back of my Grandfather's Bentley from over 50 years ago.

What are they all bleating about?

Nicky Samengo-Turner
Hundon, Suffolk

PLAYING AGAINST TYPE

SIR – In the mid 1960s my father was to marry my stepmother in Chelsea. His boss generously loaned him his convertible E-Type for the weekend so that the newlyweds could leave the registry office in style.

On the Friday evening my father proudly drove through London in the car and halted at traffic lights on the Embankment. To his astonishment two mini-skirted blondes climbed into the car and asked, 'Where are we going?'

My father said that he was going home and was

getting married next day. The girls left blowing kisses.

He often wondered whether the appeal was him or the car. I did not express an opinion.

Basil Larkins
Burgess Hill, West Sussex

THE CHICKENS THAT DIDN'T CROSS THE ROAD

SIR — I was very moved by the proposal by People for the Ethical Treatment of Animals for the erection of a permanent memorial to chickens killed in a traffic accident on the M62.

On a recent trip to Alnwick in Northumberland, I saw the following dead animals in the road: a rabbit, a hedgehog, several frogs, a squirrel, a badger, a stoat and a young deer. Since then I've been signed off work with PTSD after discovering several thousand dead flies on the windscreen and bonnet of my car.

A.C.
Newcastle upon Tyne

A MERRY CHRISTMAS

SIR – I recently purchased two breathalysers to be placed in our twenty-something children's stockings whilst they were at home with us over Christmas. Upon opening them, we were amazed to find within the packs £40 of vouchers from a well-known wine company.

R. Sherlock
Reepham, Norfolk

ADAPTING TO NEW AIRPORT SECURITY

SIR – While it seems a mockery that we should have to charge mobile phones and laptops before flying to America, I think it will be far more inconvenient to our American cousins when they find out that we have a different type of plug, meaning they will have to buy adaptors to charge their own equipment.

Is this an oversight by the 'Intelligence' agencies?

Mike Stanford-Eyre
Bishop's Stortford, Hertfordshire

SIR — I must be missing something. By asking passengers to switch on their devices at the airport, surely the risk is that as many people, if not more, would be killed?

Michael Dollin
Penn, Buckinghamshire

SIR — Why all the fuss? In the 1960s and 1970s, before the time of portable and hand-held computers, we had to show airport staff that any calculators were in working order.

Stan Jarvis
Farnham, Surrey

SIR — In 1972 I brought our newborn son back to England to visit my parents. We landed at Heathrow and I stood in front of the three possible entry points: UK and Commonwealth, EEC and 'Other'. Clutching my son's German and my British passport (no chance of him inheriting a British passport through the mother in those days), I wondered where to go.

Seeing my indecision, the cheerful immigration officer called out: 'It's alright, love, you can bring your little Kraut in this way.'

I was overjoyed to hear a real English voice and

real English humour after years of Swiss stuffiness and we had a good laugh.

In my youthful naivety I didn't realise that we were being racially abused and sexually harassed. Is it too late to make a bit of money out of it?

Penny Bohrer
Churchill, Oxfordshire

SIR – On seeing your headline, 'You won't fly if your phone is flat' my immediate thought was, thank heavens I still have a phone the shape of a Mars Bar.

Michael Cattell
Mollington, Cheshire

DEAR DAILY
TELEGRAPH

DEAR PICTURE EDITOR

SIR – As regular readers, my husband and I wonder if others are getting as tired as we are of the relentless photographs, usually on the front page, of Gwyneth Paltrow, Emma Watson, Kate Winslet and so on.

You could give us all a break from the monotony and publish a photograph like the one attached of a really beautiful female, no make-up, no designer clothes and no red carpet, just completely natural and taken on safari recently in the Kruger National Park.

Jennifer Graeme
Shaldon, Devon

SIR – Why is it that all female celebs having their photograph taken feel the urge to stand crossed-legged? Are they desperate for the lavatory?

Janie Binns
Bramhall, Cheshire

SIR — Three pictures of Esther McVey in two days — hurrah! Has she replaced the Duchess of Cambridge as your preferred totty? Thank you on behalf of the older man.

Brian Inns
Chertsey, Surrey

SIR — Please, please, no more pictures of Samantha Cameron; after all, the only reason she is well known is because she is married to our idiot Prime Minister.

B.B.
Gerrards Cross, Buckinghamshire

SIR — In the event that the Jeremy Clarkson soap opera continues to dominate the news, can we please have more on the first Mrs Clarkson?

Bharat Jashanmal
Fairford, Gloucestershire

SIR — Martin Amis asks, 'Why are we obsessed with the great British novel?' I ask, 'Why is the *Telegraph* so obsessed with Martin Amis?'

John Graham
Beckermet, Cumbria

TILL CROSS WORDS US DO PART

SIR – After 43 years of wedded bliss, it was a great shock this morning to find that my wife, for the first time, had attempted to complete the *Telegraph* crossword before me.

What should I do? Should we move to separate copies? Should I tactfully suggest that she restricts her efforts to the iPad edition? Or is divorce the inevitable conclusion?

Bob Ballingall
Farnsfield, Nottinghamshire

SIR – In the interests of marital harmony, would it be possible for you to print the Sudoku puzzles on the back of one of your large advertisements? At present I have the privilege of reading the paper first, after which I cut out the Sudoku, hand the paper to the wife and head for the study.

Unfortunately, if there is part of an interesting story missing because of my scissoring, I am met with demands for the missing piece, which is not conducive to deep thought.

Peter McPherson
Merriott, Somerset

SIR — You report that we should walk for 30 minutes every day. I venture out for a 24-minute brisk walk to collect the *Telegraph*, and on my return complete the two Sujikos and the Kakuro, without fail. Does that make up for the missing six minutes?

Malcolm Warburton
Ettiley Heath, Cheshire

SIR — Thursday's online edition supplied Friday's Cryptic Crossword, thus giving me a welcome head start over my wife, who completes the printed version.

I wonder if you would consider extending this feature to the racing results?

Stephen McWeeney
Hartburn, Northumberland

THE DAILY BECKHAM

SIR — I am sick and tired of the ****-sucking sycophancy towards David Beckham in all the British Press. How does David Beckham looking unshaven constitute 'stealing the show'?

Sir Bradley Wiggins won gold medals at three Olympics and became the first Brit to win the Tour de France. Now that's world-class sporting excellence. Better than losing in two World Cup quarter finals, isn't it?

Go and find the evidence for a true exclusive and treat your public as human beings, not misdirected junkies dreaming of David Beckham committing adultery with 12 women every day until kingdom come.

R.T.J.
Ickenham, Middlesex

SIR – I noticed that Mr Beckham had a button missing from his right sleeve cuff in the advertisement for Sky Broadband in today's paper. I can understand that Mrs Beckham may consider sewing on a button a little beneath her, but I would have thought that Mr Beckham had sufficient money to throw away any clothing in need of repair.

Robin Lloyd Owen
Medway, Kent

SIR – In today's twenty-page Sport section, seven of them headed 'Football', the only news item concerning any female was a single column on an 11-year-old girl qualifying for the US Women's Golf Open.

If I were a young sportswoman I would be frustrated to see a double-page spread devoted

to Yaya Touré's bitter feelings about a forgotten
birthday, while any success my team may have had is
nowhere to be found in your pages.

Norma Brewer
London N10

A PANICKY 2:2 IN CLIMATE
CHANGE SCIENCE

SIR — When I was an undergraduate studying
Classics at Oxford, one of my tutors, semi-jokingly,
provided us with the following tip for what to do
when flummoxed by an exam question: 'If you can't
think of anything to write, invent an early-20th-
century German scholar called Müller, assign to
him the most extreme point of view you can think
of, and argue tooth and nail against it.'

In the context of Classics, this could involve
assigning 'Müller' with the opinion that
Clytemnestra was, in fact, a devoted and loving wife.
Or that killing his daughter was the easiest decision
Agamemnon ever made. Thankfully, I never had to
use this tactic, though it was always comforting to
have it in the armoury.

Journalists reporting on the 'climate change'
debate (formerly the 'global warming' debate)
employ this tactic on a daily basis. Only their Müller

goes by the name of 'climate change deniers', referring to people who, supposedly, deny that climate ever changes, and that man can have any influence on it whatsoever.

No climate sceptic I have ever encountered has had this opinion. Real climate sceptics, of which many are eminent scientists, hold the specific view that: a) climate is less sensitive to carbon dioxide forcing than alarmist predictions make it out to be; and b) the dangers of warming are grossly exaggerated.

This view acknowledges both that climate changes and that man may play some role in influencing it; it is merely sceptical of the extent and impact of human-induced warming.

As the majority of the public doesn't understand terms such as 'forcing', 'feedbacks' or 'climate sensitivity', journalists are able to get away with Müller time and time again.

My question is: when will writers of major news organisations start writing more like professional journalists, and less like Oxford undergraduates panicking in a finals paper?

Alex Hadcock
Wolvercote, Oxfordshire

IMMORTAL, INVINCIBLE, INVISIBLE

SIR – Your City Diary takes credit for changing the line-up at the oil and gas industry's 'powerful' launch event by pointing out the lack of female faces. May I point out the lack of female faces in the *Telegraph*'s obituary column? Perhaps women of any significance never die – in which case we can look forward to them running the world in the near future.

Jennifer Charteris
Newcastle upon Tyne

SIR – Your edition of February 6, 2014 carried the obituaries of two people who died in December 2013. If you are going to report last year's news, can you revert to last year's cover price?

David Miller
Chigwell, Essex

SIR – Discussing the de-selection of MPs, your correspondent tells us that the member for Bournemouth East suffered this fate in February 1959, '45 years ago'. As one born in that year, I was pleasantly surprised that I am 45 years of age, despite feeling a little older.

Mike Finnis
Hinchley Wood, Surrey

DISAPPOINTED OF CUMBRIA

SIR – Six whole pages of L'instant Chanel adverts and no space left to mark the 150th anniversary of composer Richard Strauss? *Daily Telegraph*, you suck!

I'm not sure if this is the right expression but it feels like a modern way to say, 'Disgusted of Penrith'. Well, more disappointed really.

Ian France
Penrith, Cumbria

SIR – I appreciate that the *Telegraph* needs to take adverts to subsidise the cover price, but I did not enjoy having to struggle through pages 12 to 17 at a cramped breakfast table this morning. If this continues I will need to sign up for an advanced origami class.

Clive Pilley
Westcliff-on-Sea, Essex

SIR – You are advertising a £90 pillow to cure snoring! A gentle kick is far cheaper.

Malcolm Lukey
Nayland, Suffolk

SIR – Gadzooks! St George's Day and no mention of it in the paper! The red rose in my lapel is wilting as I write. Off with your head, sir!

Robert Vincent
Wildhern, Hampshire

SIR – In the past few weeks *The Daily Telegraph* has reported that researchers have discovered the following: fathers who are their children's main carer become as emotionally attached as the mothers; women who have husky voices are less likely to be taken on by employers; fathers who share housework have more ambitious daughters; people who eat three slices of bread per day are more likely to be obese than those who eat less; hungry men prefer plumper women (What? To eat?).

Who on earth commissions these ridiculous surveys?

Peter Whincup
Holton-le-Clay, Lincolnshire

SIR – Basking in the garden over the weekend it dawned upon me how blessed we are to live in this great country. A temperate climate; a passive spirit; cricket at Lord's; tennis at Wimbledon; sports day and the egg and spoon race; the village fete; car boot sales and real ale.

These things are in the English DNA. It is a way of life which those who seek to destroy cannot understand and yet is the very essence of why they will fail.

Sadly, these truths will not sell newspapers.

J. Kendrick
Claverley, Shropshire

A JOE KERR WRITES

SIR – I am a longstanding *Daily Telegraph* reader and regularly contribute letters to the Letters page. Quite a bit of success in getting published over the years!

However, this is not a letter but an idea for an April Fool. Recently there was a very amusing letter forum on the topic of lavatory rolls that ran for about a week. I didn't get one published this time, but the gist of it was as follows: 'In our house the upstairs loo is cold and tiled and subject to condensation so the paper hangs to the front. The downstairs loo is wood panelled, dry and cosy and the paper hangs to the back.'

This bit of nonsense got me thinking. A small news item could be put in the paper, along the lines of: 'Following a national survey a major toilet tissue manufacturer is planning to launch a toilet roll in two option packs: rolls with front drop paper and rolls with back drop paper.

'Mr Joe Kerr a spokesperson for the company said, "This innovation will give customers the option of purchasing toilet rolls to suit their own individual hanging preferences".'

What do you think? I have mentioned this prank to a few friends and they think it's a great idea.

PS Joe Kerr = Joker!!!!!!

James Logan
Portstewart, Northern Ireland

RID US OF RIDDELL'S RIDDLES

SIR – I read – somewhat unusually, I may say – Mary Riddell's article on Bob Crowe.

I quote: 'Mr Miliband may also fall short of the stereotype of a romantic icon – but compared with Mr McCluskey, his hopes of perfectibility make him a composite of Ryan Gosling and Childe Harold, with a dash of Mr Darcy thrown in.'

I'm not at all sure what on earth this pretentious twaddle is supposed to mean. Even with his classical allusions, Boris is miles ahead of this. Please give greater consideration to your readership and dispense with Ms Riddell.

R.D. Sturrock
Flackwell Heath, Buckinghamshire

GORDON'S ALIVE!

SIR — If you intend to publish any more pictures of the delightfully buxom Bryony Gordon 'en decolletage' as you did in the magazine today, would you kindly give me three days warning so that, with my advancing years, I can make sure I am sitting down and have changed the battery in my pace-maker by the time the paper arrives?

Ted Shorter
Hildenborough, Kent

SIR — Each of your many contributors has a head and shoulders photograph, apart from Bryony Gordon who, for some reason, displays a cleavage. Please will you treat her the same as everyone else.

Mrs M. Williams
Ashton-in-Makerfield, Manchester

SIR – I was so excited to see another article by Bryony Gordon, on Bryony Gordon. She has a child and a husband; how positively fascinating!

R.S.
London W10

SIR – Hooray for Bryony Gordon! She can be in my gang.

Unity Lawler
Heysham, Lancashire

LETTER-WRITING THERAPY

SIR – I always feel better when I have written a letter to the editor, even more so on the rare occasions when it is published.

However, I wonder if, say over the last fifty years, anything of significance has taken place as a direct result of any letter.

Certainly nothing from mine.

J.D. Morgan
Beaconsfield, Buckinghamshire

SIR — Surely one of the first signs of spring is when letters start appearing in papers discussing what the first signs of spring are?

Stuart Paul
Olton, West Midlands

SIR — My husband declares the arrival of spring when he has had his first sighting of a pierced navel button.

Sybil Green
Wenvoe, Glamorgan

SIR — If proof were required of the efficacy of letters to the *Telegraph* and the power of the letters page here it is: for the first time in living memory I am going to have to buy some rubber bands.

I have always depended on the postman's pavement deposits but, following your series of letters, this source has disappeared, at least here in Chingford.

Derek Pedder
Chingford, Essex

SIR – Only a reader of *The Daily Telegraph*, from
Purley-on-Thames in Berkshire, could write to
the editor giving as reason to possess a freezer: to
provide two ice cubes each evening for his wife's gin
and tonic.

Eric Marsh
Hathersage, Derbyshire

SIR – No gentleman would write a letter to the
editor of the *Telegraph*.

C.R.
Thruxton, Hampshire

SIR – Browsing through *Imagine My Surprise . . .*,
the charming little book of unpublished letters
to the *Telegraph*, I read that a correspondent finds
the Letters page a useful social networking site
and, noting the absence of regular contributors,
morbidly draws the obvious conclusion.

This troubled me as I, for one, am still here and
point out to friends that my absence is probably
because I have submitted nothing recently deemed
sufficiently interesting or witty.

Lance Warrington
Northleach, Gloucestershire

SIR – Most of my letters to this great newspaper are sent while at an espresso bar at Pulborough railway station.

John Barstow
Pulborough, West Sussex

SIR – Where do they all go? Over the years I have written many letters to your paper and none has yet appeared in print. What is the average number of rejections for any individual letter writer? Is it worth my while to keep writing in the hope that one day I shall see my letter in print? How do you choose which to print? Is there a secret format?

C.W.
Winchester, Hampshire

SIR – At last! Having read Duncan Rayner's contributions to your letters column over many years, we now discover the reason for his extensive and interesting knowledge. He is a coffee merchant.

Ivor J. Boulton
Marton, Lincolnshire

SIR — Based on Wednesday's contributions, which included letters from Robert Courtney-Harris, Anthony Harris and Mike Harris, can we expect the bottom right hand corner to be henceforth known as Harris Corner?

(Corny, I know, but I thought I would say it before Nairn Lawson of Portbury, Somerset, does so.)

John Ley-Morgan
Weston-super-Mare, Somerset

SIR — I noted with interest today that almost half of the letters printed were from readers in Dorset and Hampshire. Are there more *Telegraph* readers in these areas? Are readers here more literate? Or more aware of what's happening?

Or is your Letters Editor from Dorset/Hampshire?

Allan Dockerty
Eccleston, Lancashire

EDITING THE EDITOR

SIR – Am I the only reader to be shocked that Iain Hollingshead thinks that Norton Juxta Twycross is in Warwickshire? Surely, the journalist entrusted with the momentous task of editing the collections of unpublished *Telegraph* letters ought to be more fastidious in his research?

Norton Juxta is, of course, in Leicestershire. Royal Mail may decree a postal address for the village of 'Nuneaton, Warwickshire', but it cannot move it physically into God's Own County.

John Waine
Nuneaton, Warwickshire

THE IRREPLACEABLE MATT

SIR – The saddest phrase on my Kindle: 'Matt is on holiday'.

Sue Fentiman
Bromley, Kent

SIR – For those missing Matt may I share an image that came to me recently of him drawing cartoons in the sand on some remote beach.

Bob Stebbings
Chorleywood, Hertfordshire

P.S.

My Dear Hollingshead,

God! Man! You never give up, do you? Such stamina! Six books of rejected and therefore second-rate missives from outspoken readers, indeed!

I have visions of you on all fours in the dimly lit basement office of the Letters Editor, grey from exposure to his falling cigar ash, clasping at the scrunched-up balls of paper he casts to the threadbare carpet around his roll-top desk as he chooses the correspondence for the day. All the while you are having to dodge his flailing carpet-slippered feet as he swings himself around in his horsehair-stuffed, revolving oak chair. When you've stuffed your pullover with as much as you can, you scurry off to a disused cupboard where you are allowed to live.

It is here, to the accompaniment of the clackety-clack of the news department's elderly four-bank Royal typewriters, that you carefully smooth out each letter and pass it to your dog to flatten by lying upon it. Then, after sorting into subject piles, you creep out to borrow the office stapling machine and render each bundle secure. And hey pushto! You have compiled another book!

Good stuff, old chap, good stuff! Enterprising. I like it!

You want to use yet another letter from Ord-Hume? Of course you may! You prove yourself the discerning, wise old man of *Telegraph* Towers. If the dam' fellow in the swivel chair doesn't like my writings, then it's his loss. At least you appreciate what I turn out.

Or, on the other hand, perhaps you merely had a blank space at the end of a chapter and needed a four-and-a-half line piece of nonsense to even up the bottom margin and anything that came to hand would do.

In that case, Hollingshead, that's not good cricket, is it? I'm rather disappointed in you now.

Arthur W. J. G. Ord-Hume
Guildford, Surrey

Dear Mr Hollingshead,

Having been successful, after years of trying, in having three letters published in the newspaper over a comparatively short period, I was disappointed that my request to have a letter published in your unpublished letters book has gone unheeded.

My distress was compounded by the discovery of eight blank pages at the end of the latest edition. Perhaps these are for those of us who have been unsuccessful to fill in ourselves so that we can claim to be included in the book?

Margaret Hancock
Yateley, Hampshire